To my husband, Eddie, and my children, Korie Michelle and Scott Eric Klein,
who have always been and always will be
my anchor and life support systems,

&

To my cheering section: my parents, Marian and Daniel Heller and Anne Klein,
who have consistently and unconditionally provided me with their support,
love, and pride.

D.H.K.

To my best friend in the world and loving husband Kevin, who has been
a great source of support and laughter through
the best times and the tough times;

To my daughters, Caitlin and Cassie, who have given me
encouragement and the constant reminder of what is truly important in life;

&

To my remarkable parents, Art and Midge Watson, and my sisters, Jane and Marcy,
who always believed that I could do whatever I wanted to do with my life.

E.W.P.

# Spoken Communication for Students Who Are Deaf or Hard of Hearing:
## A Multidisciplinary Approach

Diane Heller Klein
Elizabeth Watson Parker

Butte Publications, Inc.
Hillsboro, OR  USA

# Spoken Communication for Students Who Are Deaf or Hard of Hearing:
## A Multidisciplinary Approach

Editor: Ellen Todras
Cover design and page layout: Anita Jones

Butte Publications, Inc.
P. O. Box 1328
Hillsboro, OR 97123-1328
U.S.A.

ISBN 1-884362-54-0

# Acknowledgments

We first met at a CAID conference in 2000. As we chatted, we realized that we had a lot in common personally and professionally. From being "speech teachers" and deaf educators to having two children and similar interests, we began to feel as though we had known each other for decades. When we began to exchange some of our ideas over e-mail, we were astonished to discover that our thoughts were identical! We even wondered if the other person had somehow gotten access to our computer files. But we also knew that if we were both thinking the same thing, thousands of miles apart, this must be good.

Now, several years later, we are again struck with wonder that these ideas have materialized into a book. Thrilled with a sense of accomplishment, we are equally aware that such an endeavor is accomplished only with the support of many colleagues and friends.

*Dee Klein:* Thanks to my mentor, Dr. Diane Levy Eger. Diane's constant and never-wavering faith in my abilities (and her little voice in my ear) helped more than she will ever know to complete this task. Diane is the kind of mentor who believes in you almost more than you believe in yourself.

I also thank Dr. Shari Robertson, who religiously read and scrupulously edited the first draft of the book, and Dr. Laura Marshak, who guided me through the process of getting published. Thanks is tendered to my EDHL 307 students—Rebecca Brody, Anita Fisher, Julie Flack, Jennifer Freas, Rachel Jacobson, Shannon Jackson, Julie Krause, Amanda McMillen, Angie Nordstrom, Kari Stagno, and Amanda Wysocki— who were my guinea pigs. They printed off countless revisions of each chapter for class, offering suggestions, providing thoughtful critiques, and giving the important perspective, the *student's* perspective, on the relevance and saliency of every chapter. Thanks also go out to students Christy Roth and Melissa Musselman, who provided insightful feedback on the book's cover design and color format. After all, students want a visually inviting book as well as an intellectually stimulating one!

I thank my serendipitously found "twin sister," co-author, Liz Parker. We both had the same dream and fate brought us together to make it happen. The bi-coastal writing and telephone sessions, technology challenges, and joint crash writing weekends at each other's homes have given me a friend and co-author for life. For that, I am eternally grateful.

*Liz Parker:* I wish to thank the many teachers, friends, and colleagues who taught me so much about deaf education and specifically about spoken communication skills as they relate to students who are deaf or hard of hearing. Sara Freathy was my first mentor in this great profession, followed by Chris Franco and Virginia Hecker. Dr. Jess Freeman King caused me to constantly rethink my philosophical viewpoint and together with Dr. James Blair and the deaf education faculty at Utah State University encouraged me to tackle this project. Robyn Allred and Marcy McCandless offered invaluable feedback as they read through the first drafts of the book.

Much appreciation goes to my students as well. I am grateful to the many children with whom I have worked throughout the years, who taught me that speech must be fun. I thank my graduate students for their honest feedback and willingness to remain open: DeWayne Berg, Aimee Breinholdt, Lorelyn Bruner, Lindsay Budge, Shannon Call, JaLyn Christensen, Heather Elwell, Melanie Hanny, Emily Hanson, Gina Harkness, Michael Jordan, Michelle Jordan, Teresa Kunde, Devon Kuykendall, Katie Lichfield, Clarice Luke, Jennifer Nettleton, Marci Petersen, Lori Pettit, Kelli Ross, Stacey Sessions, and Jonathan Webb. Barry Utley expressed the concept that speech may be thought of as "one tool in the tool belt," which planted the seed for the premise of the book.

Also, I want to thank my new friend and co-author, Dee Klein, for her expertise, her encouragement, and her friendship. Miles divided us, but one vision brought us together.

We both thank illustrators Saralee Manwaring for the tool belt drawing; Sara Lynn, for the ear and speech anatomy drawings in Chapters 2 and 3; and Amanda McMillen for the Cued Speech reference chart in Chapter 7.

Finally, one cannot write a book unless the support system is there to get it published. We offer most sincere thanks to our publisher, Matt Brink; editor, Ellen Todras; and designer, Anita Jones. They made the development of this text an exciting and rewarding journey to reality.

D.H.K. and E.W.P.

# Table of Contents

# *A Message to Our Readers*

Someone recently asked us if we were "ever going to be done working on that book." This comment got us thinking about the "work" we've done on this project. It never really felt like work at all. In fact, the act of gathering information, sharing what we've seen great teachers do all over the country, and proposing a new outlook to teaching spoken communication to deaf children was not a chore, but a liberating, uplifting experience.

Anyone involved with children who are deaf knows how fortunate and privileged he or she is. We didn't go into this field to work with deaf children as though it were a laborious or tedious task. And we didn't go into teaching to get rich! We got involved in deaf education because there's something that pulls us toward sharing the world around us with little ones who are just beginning to experience life. We entered this field to be with learners of all ages who have exciting lives and want to share a part of themselves with the world and become the best people that they can be.

Teachers, parents, and speech and language pathologists all want to do their best for children. Although we may not always agree on the best path to take, we can agree to keep the child's best interests first and foremost on our minds. By talking together, and by understanding divergent backgrounds, we can learn from each other and focus on the best path for each individual child.

Congratulations to the thousands of great teachers of deaf children who have helped contribute—knowingly or unknowingly—to the writing of this book. Congratulations to parents, who are their children's first heroes and first teachers. Congratulations to preservice teachers, who have watched their friends declare majors that will probably earn them more money, but who followed their hearts instead. Congratulations to speech and language pathologists, who teach deaf children and are willing to learn new techniques to enhance their practices. Congratulations to all teachers in this fine profession who aren't afraid of trying new things. As you start a new school year, look out at the fresh new faces in your classroom with renewed resolve: you're not "working," you're teaching. You are one of the fortunate few who are able to touch lives in an exceptional and unique way.

D.H.K. and E.W.P.

# *Part I*

# Foundations for Understanding

# Introduction to Part I

*Spoken Communication for Students Who Are Deaf and Hard of Hearing: A Multidisciplinary Approach* is written for everyone involved in the education of deaf and hard of hearing students.

## Teachers of Deaf and Hard of Hearing Students

Specially trained teachers of students who have any type or degree of hearing loss are, at some point during the educational day, responsible for assisting the child with his or her spoken language skills. The teachers model the appropriate spoken English patterns and provide opportunities for spoken communication practice. They need to be ready to facilitate communication in all of its forms across all curricular areas.

## General Education Teachers

The vast majority of children who have hearing loss go to school in regular education settings (Johnson, 2002). The school may be the regular neighborhood school or a school in a neighboring district. The student will likely be in a classroom with primarily hearing children and with a general education teacher who has little or no knowledge of working with a child who has hearing loss. Just as the general education teacher's special education counterpart is required to assist with spoken communication, so must the general education teacher be prepared to help the child when needed.

## Speech and Language Pathologists

Regardless of educational placement, the child who is deaf or hard of hearing very often works with a speech and language pathologist (SLP). Speech and language pathologists have extensive training in developing speech and correcting speech and language errors that occur in people who have hearing. In general, SLPs do not receive training to work with children who have hearing loss. It is crucial for the SLP to understand and apply speech reception and speech production principles from the perspective of the child with hearing loss.

## Parents

Finally, there are no people more important in a child's life than his or her parents. The job of parenting is hard enough without adding the need to understand what goes into simply communicating with your child. Yet, parents of children with hearing loss do need to understand why their child is having both the receptive and expressive communication difficulties they encounter. They also need to feel comfortable with using strategies that will help their child become more facile spoken communication users.

For any of these individuals—the teacher of deaf children, general education teacher, SLP, or parent—a lack of understanding of the principles of spoken communication can have permanent negative impact on the child's speech abilities. Knowledge of the basic principles of spoken communication can and will help to ensure that the assistance the child receives is appropriate and helpful.

# Book Purpose

Part I of this book, "Foundations for Understanding," provides the basic background knowledge needed to understand both the receptive and expressive attributes of spoken communication. It is not intended to provide comprehensive information. For students in teacher preparation programs, SLPs, and teachers of deaf and hard of hearing children, these chapters should function as a review of previously learned materials. For the general education teacher and parent, the information in the following chapters is intended to give a picture of what is involved anatomically and physiologically in spoken communication.

Part II, "Applications," shows how to maximize the strengths of the various members of the team, how to make the most of tightly scheduled classrooms, how to recognize the skills of parents as valued team members, and how to work together in collaboration toward a common goal. Part II provides suggestions for incorporating spoken communication activities into all of the daily school routines. We do not focus on the drill-and-practice activities typically assigned to speech classes.

# Conventions

As educators who have worked for a combination of 50+ years with children who have hearing loss, we feel strongly that respect for the child is one of our highest priorities. Using "person first" language in writing is one means of showing respect. In this book, we use *child who has hearing loss* and *deaf and hard of hearing child* interchangeably out of respect for both the child and the Deaf community. We often use the abbreviation *D/HH* for *deaf and hard of hearing* to facilitate reading ease. We also alternate, chapter by chapter, the use of *he* and *she* (and *his* and *her*) to promote gender equity. Our children are not gender-neutral; we do not want to refer to them as such. We interchange the use of *SLP* with *speech and language teacher* because children, parents, and other professionals often view the SLP in an educational setting as the speech teacher.

In Chapter 1, we will discuss the roles of each member of the multidisciplinary team. We often refer to the reader in the second person *you* because we want *you*, the reader, to feel as though you are part of an informational dialogue. This book is written for *you*. We also choose to use the term *spoken communication* rather than *speech production*. Speech is but one aspect of the overall language and communication picture, but it is the term that is most often used when referring to spoken communication skills. We want to encourage the readers to think about speech as spoken language or spoken communication; the terms are both used to facilitate that vocabulary shift.

We periodically present a "not-so-hypothetical" situation for consideration and discussion to highlight various chapter concepts. Some of these scenarios come from personal experiences, and others are a compilation of several typical situations. Some veteran teachers will read these Not-So-Hypotheticals and nod their heads in agreement as they recall similar experiences in their own teaching. New teachers and teachers in training need to be aware that these situations will undoubtedly come up in their careers in the future. Parents will notice similarities with their own child and understand that they are not alone. Not-So-Hypotheticals appear throughout the book in boxes, set in a different type.

At the beginning of each chapter you will find an outline of the contents for the chapter. The outline is provided as a means for you to pre-conceptualize the information and to assist you in organizing your thoughts and notes. Finally, the book's appendices serve a variety of functions—from providing more information about available resources, to supplying possible handouts for parents and teachers, to offering inserts for a student Communication Book.

# Outcomes

As you read through this book, you will gain a better understanding of all that goes into the process of becoming a user of spoken communication. In Part I you will understand the anatomy and physiology involved in speech production. In Part II you will learn strategies for developing and enhancing spoken communication in a classroom or group setting. You will also receive information enabling parents to become integral members of the team, as well as additional information on resources and technology suggestions to enhance your program.

After reading this book you will become advocates for the concept that *all* members of the team are speech teachers for our D/HH children. The responsibility belongs to everyone. By working as a multidisciplinary team, we will achieve positive spoken communication outcomes for our children.

# *Chapter 1*

# **Why a New Speech Book?**

Why do we need a new book on spoken communication? Because we believe that every child, regardless of the type or degree of hearing loss, or the mode of communication used, has the ability and the right to establish some level of spoken language skill. There is power in words in all modes of communication, and children need the tools to harness that power.

> Kelsey is twelve years old. She was born with a profound bilateral hearing loss. Kelsey has always depended on her family to help her get the things she needs because she hates to write notes. Today, she walked into the 7-Eleven without her brother for the first time ever. She walked up to a clerk and asked, "Where can I find batteries?" To her absolute delight, he smiled and told her where to find them.

Kelsey is a bright young lady. She knew that by writing notes, she could obtain things from people who did not know sign language. She also didn't want to always depend upon writing notes so she took a stab at using her spoken communication skills. They weren't perfect, but they were sufficient for the clerk to respond to her question.

> Donovan is three years old. His severe bilateral sensorineural hearing loss was not detected until he was two years old. His mom said he pointed at everything he wanted even after they started signing with him. When he talked with his immediate family, signing really helped, along with pointing. Today, he had a baby-sitter who didn't know any signs. She was having trouble understanding what he was asking for; he yelled, "Wan tooty!" and she suddenly "got it." "Oh, you want a cookie! Okey dokey! Here you are." Donovan was quite pleased with himself; he got his cookie!

Donovan certainly had the power of communication with his family using sign, but it was the use of spoken language with an unfamiliar person that helped him achieve his objective. Donovan may never be able to say that phrase any better in his life, but he still understood the power of spoken language as a tool and used it to the best of his ability to meet his needs.  Kelsey and Donovan gained in the confidence necessary to capture and control the tool of spoken language.

# Developing Spoken Communication

For any language to develop, a child must first have a reason to communicate. Donovan wanted that cookie. Eventually he tried every method of communication he knew to obtain his desired objective. In addition to a reason for communicating, there must also be a nurturing and safe environment for normal mistakes to be made and naturally modified. It is also essential that a complete model be provided for the child in all of his environments. Spoken language abilities are not developed through pullout models of speech instruction in the schools or by drill-and-practice strategies used at home.

Unfortunately, many deaf adults look back on their experience with spoken communication very negatively. Some resent all of the drill-and-practice sessions, and being pulled out of classroom activities. Others believe their efforts were constantly being corrected and seldom understood. In many cases they perceived their entire education as negative because of the demand for perfection from some teachers. We cannot afford to have another generation of deaf adults who feel invalidated when recalling their attempts at spoken communication. This negative attitude about speech training within the Deaf community causes bad feelings about deaf education as a whole. As teachers, speech language pathologists, and parents, we must do everything we can to ensure that these negative feelings do not persevere.

In the development of spoken language, parents should never have to "go it alone," and the child's early intervention specialist, classroom or deaf education teachers, or SLP should not territorially assume primary responsibility for a child developing communication skills. It *must* be a team effort!

Historically, each of the professionals who worked with the child focused only on his particular area of expertise, pulling the child in a number of unconnected directions (Figure 1.1). Although speech and language pathologists have extensive training in diagnosing articulation and speech errors in hearing children, they generally receive little or no training in sign language or teaching speech to D/HH children. Likewise, teachers of the deaf receive some speech instruction in their teacher preparation programs, but the emphasis is usually on teaching methods and strategies in the content areas, not in speech for their students. Parents know their children best but are not prepared to teach them speech when hearing loss is present. Although all mean well, more often than not, the children are caught in the middle.  It is time for a change in the traditional instructional model of teaching speech to

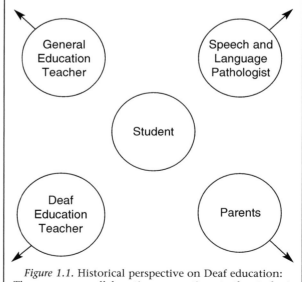

*Figure 1.1.* Historical perspective on Deaf education: There were no collaborative connections to the student.

deaf children; it is time for all parties to work together. Figure 1.2 shows how a multidisciplinary team effort assists the child in the development of spoken language skills.

## The Multidisciplinary Team

What is meant by a multidisciplinary team approach? This is a process by which team members relinquish territoriality and become engaged in an interactive, coordinated process to successfully develop, maintain, and enhance spoken language. Current educational best practices clearly demonstrate that collaboration between professionals and parents better meets the needs of all students. Team members may differ according to

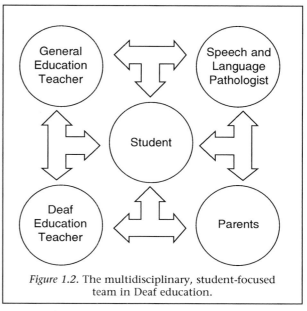

*Figure 1.2.* The multidisciplinary, student-focused team in Deaf education.

specific situations, but generally the multidisciplinary team should include 1) the classroom teachers, 2) the speech pathologist, 3) the parents, and 4) the student.

### The Teachers
Teachers of deaf children have extensive knowledge regarding the communication needs of the students in their charge. The teacher-student bond is generally a strong and positive one. Deaf education teachers are also skilled in the ability to adapt curriculum to meet those communication needs.

General education teachers have multiple teaching opportunities to incorporate spoken communication activities into daily classroom routines. They, too, have the time to develop a strong and positive relationship with the deaf or hard of hearing student.

### The SLP
Speech and language pathologists have a wide array of skills in developing phonetic and phonologic speech production. Their background is rich in evaluating, identifying, and developing individualized speech programs for children. They are accustomed to being team players and working with professionals in a variety of settings.

### The Parents
Parents are the ultimate experts regarding their child's strengths and needs. They have firsthand knowledge of the child's daily experiences. They know their child best and want what's best for him. We must encourage parents to feel comfortable coming to the table and talking about ways they can naturally enhance their child's spoken communication skills. We do not want them to go home and create a setting that requires military-like drill-and-practice periods. Parents are important key players in this collaborative team.

## The Student

The student, depending on his age, can also be a vital member of the team. The student's motivation and commitment to spoken communication significantly contributes to the success of any program. It is essential to allow the student the opportunity to express his own needs regarding his means of communication. Any spoken communication activity can easily be adapted to meet the needs of the student. He is, after all, the real consumer.

Teachers, SLPs, parents, and students must have common goals and be willing to share strategies to ensure continuity and consistency in a communication program. It is also critical that they trust one another and respect each other's unique contributions. Everyone in the child's environment can be a speech teacher. The entire team must believe that the student's efforts are worthwhile in order to be productive and to enable him to develop his best possible spoken communication skills.

For your consideration of the importance of a multidisciplinary team approach, read about Daniel in this Not-So-Hypothetical situation:

---

**Not-So-Hypothetical**

Daniel was an eleven-year-old, profoundly deaf student enrolled in the state school for the deaf, in a self-contained classroom housed in a public elementary school. Daniel was very bright, and had a wonderfully supportive family and many friends. When Daniel was younger, his parents requested that speech goals be added to his Individual Education Plan, or IEP. Throughout the years, some of his classroom teachers encouraged speech tutoring, but most did not give it much weight. Daniel was happy and doing well in school, so speech moved progressively lower down the priority list.

At this year's IEP meeting, however, Daniel's parents initiated a new push for speech, because this time, the request came from Daniel himself. The parents were much more determined to have their requests heard and would not settle for lip service any longer.

Daniel's IEP team included his parents, two team teachers, and the local speech and language pathologist, who volunteered to attend from the school district.

The teachers wanted Daniel to have speech therapy but did not want him pulled out of class, as there were already too many interruptions. The teachers would not agree to teach speech themselves, since they did not believe they had adequate skills to be speech instructors. The SLP agreed to take Daniel for tutoring although she had never worked with a deaf child before and knew no sign language.

---

Clearly, none of the options would be considered ideal. All of the professionals in the IEP meeting had expertise in different areas. Because of the inability or lack of cooperation between professionals, Daniel's speech goals were never met with any degree of satisfaction. While Daniel continues to make excellent progress in his education, his communication skills would likely be stronger had the team members been more willing to work together. An IEP team meeting is, by definition, a collaborative effort, but the type of breakdown illustrated above exists throughout the country in varying degrees. By truly working as a multidisciplinary team, with the child at the center of their focus, the participants will find several viable solutions available, and a much better outcome will ensue.

# Summary

This chapter describes the need for each member of the multidisciplinary team to work together in order for optimal success to occur. The multidisciplinary team approach may be viewed as a puzzle with many pieces. By placing all of the collaborative team pieces together, the student is supported on all sides. Contributing members of the team include the deaf education teacher, the general education teacher, the speech and language pathologist, the parents, and the students themselves.

In communicating effectively, we use written language, spoken communication, sign language, body language, facial expressions, and so on. Spoken communication may be seen as one useful tool in a communication tool bag. Some students use spoken communication as their primary tool while others use it as a secondary tool. If a student goes out into the world with only one or two tools in his tool bag, he may not be fully equipped to face the many situations he will encounter on a daily basis. Rather than encouraging one method to the exclusion of all others, we promote the strengthening of every aspect of a child's communication abilities. With a well-stocked tool bag, he will face all communication encounters with more confidence and be better prepared to succeed in the world (Figure 1.3).

*Figure 1.3.* Deaf or hard of hearing students equipped with a well-stocked communication tool bag.

# Chapter 1 Topics for Discussion

1.  Who are the significant members of a D/HH child's communication team, and what does each person bring to the table in terms of experience?

2.  Consider Daniel's Not-So-Hypothetical scenario. Identify the issues that got in the way of effective collaboration and suggest strategies to remediate the situation.

3.  At what age do you believe a child should become part of the IEP/communication planning team?  Why?

*Chapter 2*

# Foundations of Hearing

Before you can work with a child who has hearing loss, you must understand how hearing functions. It is also necessary to recognize the impact that hearing loss has on speech development. This chapter will provide the information required for you to understand the basic anatomy and physiology of the hearing mechanism. In addition, we will discuss the impact that anatomy and physiology problems have on the hearing process, and the impact hearing loss has on speech development.

## Types of Hearing Loss

Hearing loss can be physical, neurological, perceptual, or any combination of these. The type of hearing loss depends upon the location of the breakdown in the anatomy of the ear (Figure 2.1), the involvement of the Vestibulocochlear Nerve (also known as the Auditory Nerve), or the integrity of the temporal lobe of the brain. Hearing loss is typically divided into four types: conductive, sensorineural, mixed, and central losses.

**Conductive** hearing loss involves the outer and middle ear components of the ear structure. In a conductive hearing loss, sound cannot move, or be conducted, from the outside environment through the outer two parts of the ear.

**Sensorineural** hearing loss involves the inner ear structures. In a sensorineural loss, the initial nerve receptors and transmitters are not functioning because of some form of damage. The damage can be physical or chemical; the outcome is the same. The nerves are unable to transmit the electrochemical signal to the Vestibulocochlear (Auditory) Nerve and ultimately to the brain.

A **mixed** hearing loss is a combination of both a conductive and sensorineural component in the same ear. For example, a child may have a

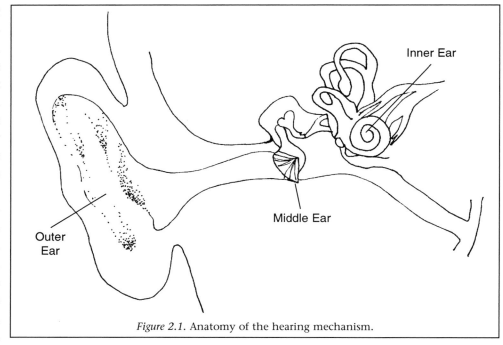

*Figure 2.1.* Anatomy of the hearing mechanism.

sensorineural hearing loss, but also have chronic otitis media (a middle ear infection), which adds a conductive component to the loss.

A **central** hearing loss is one that involves any part of the neural transmission of the sound to the brain or the temporal lobe of the brain.

# Anatomy and Physiology of Hearing

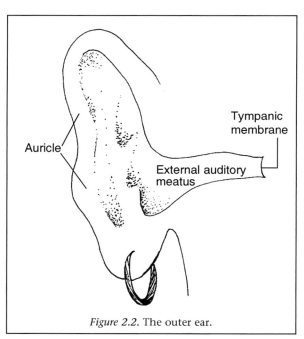

*Figure 2.2.* The outer ear.

## Outer Ear

Figure 2.2 illustrates several distinct components to the outer ear anatomy. The outermost feature of the external ear is the pinna or auricle. The auricle actually serves little purpose in the hearing process. It may collect some sound waves but the loss of the auricle does not result in any appreciable hearing loss (consider Vincent van Gogh). The external auditory meatus or canal begins on the outer side surface of the head at the auricle and proceeds inward in a slightly *s*-shaped form for about one inch. The canal focuses the sound waves down toward the tympanic membrane or eardrum. Any blockage in the ear canal causes a loss in sound conduction. Children put small toys in their ears, swimmers often get an inflammatory infection in the canal (swimmer's ear or external otitis), and everybody produces earwax, which can become impacted. In each of these situations, sound cannot reach the eardrum and that produces a conductive hearing loss.

## Middle Ear

The canal ends at the tympanic membrane or eardrum. The tympanic membrane is the beginning of the middle ear structure (Figure 2.3). The tympanic membrane is like a taut skin on the top of a drum. Its purpose is to move sound vibrations to the small bones (ossicles) in the middle ear. The ossicles are the smallest bones in the body and are amazingly resilient when you consider that they are moving whenever a sound of any type is present. The ossicles form a chain of bones that facilitate the transmission of sound. The three ossicles are the malleus (hammer), incus (anvil), and stapes (stirrup). The malleus is attached to the tympanic membrane. When sound waves reach the membrane, it begins to vibrate and that vibration begins the movement of the ossicles. This is a mechanical process of moving sound. The middle ear cavity also con-

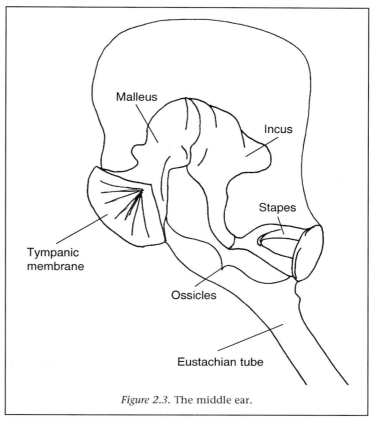

*Figure 2.3.* The middle ear.

tains the Eustachian tube, which connects the middle ear to the nasal portion of the throat. The Eustachian tube serves as an aeration device, a pressure equalizer, and a drainage tube. Unfortunately, it also serves as a means of transmitting bacteria and viruses to the middle ear. The middle ear should be filled with air; this allows sound to travel across the ossicles.

There can be many problems in the middle ear. These problems also result in conductive hearing losses because the sound is unable to be transmitted or conducted to the inner ear. A respiratory infection can cause inflammation in the Eustachian tube, or infection can spread to the middle ear cavity. When the middle ear fills with fluid (otitis media), that reduces sound transmission. A sudden trauma to the head can damage the ossicles; dislocations and fractures can occur. Heredity can also play a factor in middle ear hearing loss. A hereditary condition called otosclerosis causes the stapes to become fixed in a portion of the inner ear. Once the stapes cannot move, sound can no longer be transmitted to the inner ear. Any of these difficulties in the middle ear cavity will result in a conductive hearing loss.

Fortunately, nearly all of the problems that might occur in the outer and middle ear structures can be addressed. External otitis can be treated with medications, earwax can be removed, and perforated eardrums can heal. Middle ear infections can be treated, fractured or dislocated ossicles can be repaired, and the stapes can be released or replaced to alleviate the effects of otosclerosis. It is important to remember, however, that there may be some byproduct to any repair. When a perforated eardrum heals, scar tissue often forms on the eardrum. Middle ear infections can be chronic, which can damage the middle ear structures over time. So, even though many of these conductive problems can be reduced, there is always a strong possibility that a small conductive hearing loss may continue to exist.

## Inner Ear

The footplate of the stapes fits into the oval window, which is the entrance to the third anatomical   component of the ear, the inner ear (Figure 2.4). The inner ear begins at the vestibular system, which is comprised of three semicircular canals that are filled with fluid. These canals lie in three different planes and are at right angles to each other; they help to control a person's sense of balance. The cochlea, which is immediately below the semicircular canals, is a fluid-filled snail-shaped organ that contains nerve fibers or hair cells, which send electrical stimulation to the brain.

The cochlea has two and a half turns from the base end to the apex or pointed end of the shell shape. The fluid moves

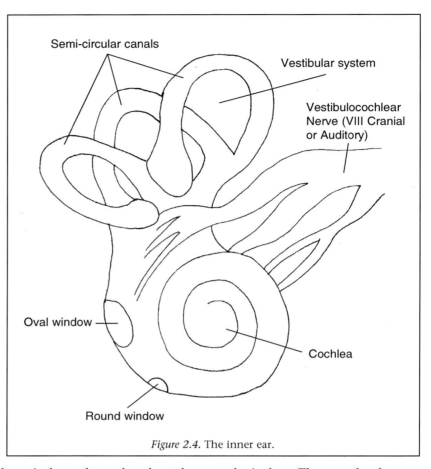

*Figure 2.4.* The inner ear.

from the oval window, through the spiral canals, and ends at the round window. Thousands of nerve fibers are lined up along the canal in the cochlea. The bones of the middle ear conduct sound to the inner ear by moving the footplate of the stapes in the oval window. That sets up a wave in the fluid that is in the inner ear. The wave moves across the nerve fibers. These nerve fibers turn the wave motion into electrical energy, which is sent along the Vestibulocochlear (Auditory) Nerve to the brain. The sound that is sent depends upon where the wave stimulates the hair cells. If the sound has a high pitch, the base of the cochlea is stimulated. If it has a low pitch, the apex end of the cochlea is stimulated.

As in other sections of the ear, a variety of problems can occur in the inner ear. Some medicines can have an ototoxic, or poisonous, effect on the inner ear and can damage the hair cells. Loud noise, such as highly amplified music, the sound of a jet engine, or repeated exposure to gunfire, can also permanently damage the hair cells. Fistulas, or small holes in the cochlear wall or semicircular canals, can cause the fluid to leak from these structures, leading to a problem in the fluid movement through the inner ear. Reduced or interrupted fluid movement affects the sensory stimulation of hearing.  Chronic vertigo, or problems with balance, can have a negative impact on hearing. Aging causes changes in the cochlea, which also produce hearing loss. Hearing loss that occurs in the inner ear is a sensorineural loss and cannot be changed through surgery or other forms of intervention. A sensorineural loss typically results in permanent hearing loss.

## Neural Ear

The fourth part of the hearing mechanism is sometimes referred to as the neural ear (Palmer, 1993). This part of hearing involves the nerve impulses that are sent to the brain and ultimately recognized as sound (Figure 2.5). The Vestibulocochlear (Auditory) Nerve has two branches. One branch connects to the vestibular area of the inner ear, and the second branch connects to the cochlea. The hair cells in the cochlea send electrical impulses to the Vestibulocochlear Nerve. Through a series of complex neural pathways where nerve fibers pass through various sections of the brain, sound is transmitted to the temporal lobe of the brain's cortex, where it is perceived or recognized as sound. Any problem that occurs along the neural pathway is called a central hearing loss.

Lesions, tumors, head trauma, ototoxic drug reaction, and vascular diseases are a few of the problems that can occur along the neural pathways. Two forms of central hearing loss that are being identified and seen more frequently in school programs are Central Auditory Processing Disorders (CAPD) and auditory neuropathy. In both of these disorders, the conduction and sensory reception components of the hearing mechanism and hearing process are in working order. The problems occur in the neural integration or transmission of sound (auditory neuropathy) or cognitive perception of sound (Central Auditory Processing Disorder). It is important to note that a hearing aid is of little benefit in central hearing loss (Gelfand, 2001).

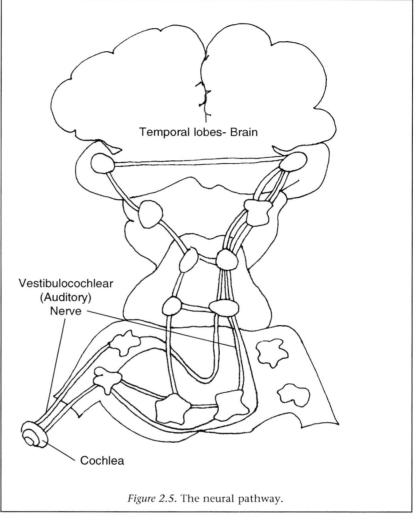

*Figure 2.5.* The neural pathway.

## Reviewing Anatomy and Physiology of Hearing

To summarize, we identified four areas of hearing anatomy: the outer ear, middle ear, inner ear, and neural ear. We reviewed the anatomical and physiological components of each part of the ear. In addition, examples of problems that impact each component were identified. The types of hearing loss that are associated with each section of the ear were also discussed.

Appendix A provides the same anatomical drawings of the hearing mechanism as are found in this chapter, but in the appendix, the body parts are not labeled. Use the drawings in the appendix as teaching tools to help students identify parts of the ear.

# Measuring Hearing Loss

An audiologist, a professional trained in the science of hearing, has a battery of diagnostic tools available to evaluate the extent of a hearing loss and recommend habilitative and rehabilitative strategies. Among these tools is the **audiometer,** a machine used to perform one form of hearing testing. The results of these tests are plotted on a graph called an audiogram.

An **audiogram** is a graphic representation of both the loudness and pitch of different sounds. Pitch is measured in Hertz (Hz) or cycles per second. The pitch is located horizontally across the top of the audiogram beginning with the low pitch. The loudness, which is measured in decibels (dB), is

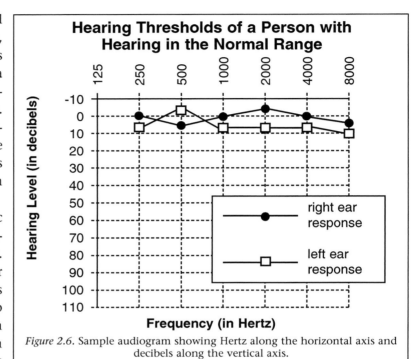

*Figure 2.6.* Sample audiogram showing Hertz along the horizontal axis and decibels along the vertical axis.

located vertically along the left side of the audiogram, beginning with zero dB. Figure 2.6 shows the audiogram of a person with hearing in the normal range.

## Air and Bone Conduction Testing

An audiologist performs air and bone conduction testing to help determine the type of hearing loss. Both conductive and sensorineural hearing losses can be identified through this type of testing.

During air and bone conduction testing, a person wears a headphone and listens to a series of tones (frequencies or pitches). The human ear can detect from 20–20,000 Hz (tones), but only the tones between 250 Hz and 8000 Hz are tested because these are the frequencies that fall within the speech range.

The tones are presented at an easily detected loudness level (decibels) at first, then at progressively softer levels until they are barely heard. Humans vary greatly in their tolerance for loud sounds. Typically, a person with normal hearing can hear and tolerate tones presented from 0 dB SPL (sound pressure level) through 100 dB SPL before it becomes uncomfortable.

## Middle Ear Measures

Another type of measurement is acoustic immittance. Immittance measures, such as tympanometry or acoustic reflex, are used to confirm conductive and sensorineural losses and to aid in the diagnosis of central hearing loss. These tests involve placing a soft rubber probe in the ear canal and introducing tones or bursts of air into the canal. These tests measure the flexibility of the eardrum, the acoustic reflex of the muscles controlling the ossicles, and other involuntary physiologic responses to a sound stimulus.

## Physiological Measures

Physiological measurements, such as auditory brainstem response or auditory evoked potentials, are used to identify central losses occurring in the neural pathway. These tests involve the placement of electrodes on an individual's skull or cochlea. Electronic "clicks" are presented through the electrodes, and the response of the Vestibulocochlear (Auditory) Nerve to these clicks is recorded in a manner similar to an electrocardiogram. A series of waveforms is produced on a graph. The size and shape of the waveforms present a diagnostic picture of the involuntary response of the neural pathway to auditory stimulation.

## Behavioral Measures

Behavioral measures, or site-of-lesion tests, are used to further define the nature and location of hearing discrepancy. These tests involve an individual responding voluntarily to a series of listening activities. A person may indicate when a sound becomes too loud to tolerate or how long it takes to stop hearing the presentation of a tone. The product of these tests is entirely dependent upon the behavioral response of the person taking the test.

## Speech Audiometry

Speech audiometry tests allow the audiologist to determine how the individual actually perceives speech sounds, which aids in the diagnosis of Central Auditory Processing Disorder (CAPD). During speech audiometry, a person repeats a series of words presented at a predetermined loudness level. The results of the test indicate how well a person discriminates the words heard. Another speech audiometry test involves determining a speech reception threshold. That is the softest point at which three spondee words (words that have two syllables with equal stress, such as *baseball* or *pitchfork)* are repeated correctly. These tests allow the audiologist to determine if there may be some form of perceptual component to the hearing loss.

Once the type of loss is diagnosed, a degree or severity is also assigned. A loss may range from a slight impairment to a profound impairment. Table 2.1 shows the audiological classifications of degrees of hearing loss.

For a more thorough description of the various hearing tests, *Essentials in Audiology* by Stanley A. Gelfand (2001) is an excellent resource.

***Table 2.1.*
**Audiological classifications of degrees of hearing loss.**

| Average hearing level | Type of loss |
| --- | --- |
| 0 –15 dB | Normal range |
| 15 – 25 dB | Slight hearing loss |
| 25 – 30 dB | Mild hearing loss |
| 30 – 50 dB | Moderate hearing loss |
| 50 – 70 dB | Severe hearing loss |
| 70+ dB | Profound hearing loss |

Note: From *Hearing in Children*, 5th Edition (p. 21), by J. L. Northern and M. P. Downs, 2002, Baltimore: Lippincott Williams & Wilkins. Copyright 2002 by Lippincott Williams & Wilkins. Adapted with permission.

# Impact of Hearing Loss on Speech Development

What impact does hearing loss have on speech development? The impact can be far-reaching or relatively minor. There is no rule-of-thumb that easily guides a teacher, speech pathologist, or audiologist in determining what impact a particular type or degree of hearing loss might have on any single child. Certain predictions, however, can be made based on what we know about the acoustic properties of speech sounds. Table 2.2 shows the progressive impact of hearing loss on speech development.

A mild hearing loss affects the ability to hear lower intensity sounds. In an extremely noisy environment, there may be some difficulty hearing soft speech (speech that is produced at less than 60 dB). Children with chronic middle ear infections often have ongoing mild hearing loss during their developmental years. This can have an impact on the development of speech sounds that are in the higher frequencies, such as the *f* or *s* sounds. It may also impact a child's ability to hear the less intense sounds at the ends of words that usually indicate plurals or past tense. Missing these sounds will influence a child's ability to understand and to some degree, produce these sounds.

**Table 2.2.**
**Impact of hearing loss on speech development.**

| Average hearing level | What can be heard without amplification | Handicapping effects if not treated within 12 months |
|---|---|---|
| 0 –15 dB (normal) | All speech sounds | None |
| 15 – 25 dB (slight) | Vowel sounds heard clearly; may miss unvoiced consonant sounds | Mild auditory dysfunction in language learning |
| 25 – 30 dB (mind) | Only some speech sounds; the louder voiced sounds | Auditory learning dysfunction; mild language retardation, mild speech problems, inattention |
| 30 – 50 dB (moderate) | Almost no speech sounds at normal conversational level | Speech problems, language retardation, learning dysfunction, inattention |
| 50 – 70 dB (severe) | No speech sounds at normal conversational levels | Severe speech problems, language retardation, learning dysfunction, inattention |
| 70+ dB (profound) | No speech or other sounds | Severe speech problems, language retardation, learning dysfunction, inattention |

*Note:* From *Hearing in Children,* 5th Edition (p. 21), by J. L. Northern and M. P. Downs, 2002, Baltimore: Lippincott Williams & Wilkins. Copyright 2002 by Lippincott Williams & Wilkins. Adapted with permission.

As a hearing loss becomes progressively more severe, a child will have a significantly more difficult time receiving auditory input of speech that is not distorted in some way. Even with the use of a hearing aid, some element of distortion will always be present. Speech production, then, has the potential to also become significantly distorted. Groups of sounds are often completely omitted from a child's repertoire. The acoustically high frequency sounds such as *s* and *sh* are included in this group. These sounds are also among some of the most common in the English language. Vowel sounds are often misperceived when their acoustic properties are within the range that a child cannot hear. A child who cannot hear or does not perceive these sounds will produce speech that, to some degree, may be unintelligible.

A word of caution: there are children who have profound hearing losses who have extremely intelligible speech. There is much more that goes into intelligible speech production for D/HH children than the acoustic response levels of a hearing loss.

# Summary

This chapter provided the basic information necessary to understand the anatomy and physiology of hearing. There are four distinct physical areas involved in hearing: the outer ear, middle ear, inner ear, and neural ear. A breakdown in any one of these systems can significantly impact the ability to receive and perceive sound.

In addition, we discussed the types of tests that measure hearing loss, types of hearing loss, and the impact hearing loss has on the production of speech. Hearing loss is as individual in nature as a child's personality. We should not make predictions about a child's potential for success in spoken communication based only on her type or degree of hearing loss. One child may have a profound hearing loss yet still make remarkable use of the little hearing that remains. Another child may have only a moderate level hearing loss, but be unable to use her hearing effectively.

Recognizing that this information can be confusing, and to facilitate your further understanding of some of these concepts, two hands-on activities have been provided after the chapter discussion questions.

# Chapter 2 Topics for Discussion

1. Using the blank anatomy picture of the ear in Appendix A, label each part of the ear's anatomy and state the function for each part.

2. Identify at least three types of hearing tests and define the component of hearing that each examines.

3. Why do you think you have to complete separate tests for speech audiometry? Support your opinion.

4. Is it possible to have conductive, sensorineural, and central hearing loss at the same time? What symptoms would a person with this combination of losses present?

# Activity #1

## Sound Waves in the Cochlea

**Supplies:**
- Opaque plastic tubing (as wide a circumference as you can get—available in a hardware or crafts store) (cochlea)
- Shredded mylar (hair cells)
- Plastic wrap (cochlear membranes)
- Water-resistant glue
- A large pan of water (at least twice the size of the tube) (perilymph)

**What to do:**
- Straighten out the mylar shreds and cut them to about one-half the diameter of the tube in length.
- Cut the tubing along one side and spread open.
- Glue the mylar strips in a straight line along the inside of one side of the tube and let the glue dry. Glue the other end to a piece of plastic wrap.
- Close up the tube. The plastic wrap should be hanging toward the middle of the tube.
- Lay the tube in a large pan of water.
- Create "sound waves" in the pan of water and observe how the hair cells (mylar strands) move in the cochlea (tube) in response to the different waves sent through the water (perilymph). (Faster/smaller waves will make the hair cells at the opening of the tube move, and slower/larger waves will move hair cells farther down the tube.)

# Activity #2

## Transmission of Neural Impulses

**Supplies:**
- A lantern battery
- Copper electrical wire
- Styrofoam balls (10 small)
- 2 lantern light bulbs
- Plastic straws
- Modeling clay

## What to do:

Give the students a copy of the neural pathway drawing from Appendix A, and have them replicate the neural pathway that the Vestibulocochlear (Auditory) Nerve takes to reach the auditory cortex of the brain. Ask them to identify what they believe each item represents.

- The lantern battery is the cochlea, and the terminals on top are the Vestibulocochlear Nerve from the right ear and left ear.
- The copper wire is the nerve fibers.
- The styrofoam balls represent each of the connection points along the neural pathway.
- The straws form the pathway and the point in the brain where the nerve fibers cross over to the other side.
- The light bulbs are the auditory cortex locations on the brain.
- Use the modeling clay to shape a brain.

If the students wire their brain correctly, they will light up both light bulbs. If there are any breaks in the connection, the sound will not be perceived by the brain!

## Alternate idea:

The instructor prepares a series of models as instructed above. However, the instructor creates breaks in the neural pathway of each model. Each model should have a different breakdown point. Put the students into small groups and instruct them to locate the breaks in the pathway (where the neural transmission is breaking down and not being transmitted). Each group should then answer the following questions:

1. What is the location of the breakdown?

2. What is the impact of a breakdown at this point along the neural pathway on the ability to perceive sound?

3. What would an audiogram with this type of problem look like?

4. What kind of hearing tests might an audiologist give to a person with this problem to confirm the loss?

5. What can be done for this type of problem?

# *Chapter 3*

# Foundations of Speech Production

Why speech? This question is asked far too often when discussing the communication needs of deaf and hard of hearing children. Depending upon the perspective of the team member, intelligible spoken communication may be considered a goal that is not obtainable by children with profound hearing loss. Is that an accurate perspective? As we have noted in previous chapters, children with hearing loss are a significantly heterogeneous group. It is impossible to state unequivocally that because a child has a profound hearing loss, he will be unable to develop intelligible spoken communication skills. In fact, there are far too many individuals with profound hearing loss who *do* develop highly intelligible speech to even ask, "Why speech?"

The question then becomes, how does one develop intelligible spoken communication abilities? In order to answer that question, it is necessary to understand the anatomy and physiology that make up the speech production process. In addition, it is important to have a basic understanding of how speech production relates to communication and English language acquisition. This chapter is not meant to be an in-depth examination of these issues. Rather, it will guide you through the production aspects of spoken communication and provide you with a basis upon which decisions can be made regarding the development of speech skills in the classroom.

# Anatomy of Speech Production

Speech begins in the lungs. Air is released from the lungs, travels up through the trachea, and reaches the vocal cords housed in the larynx. The vocal cords open as the air pushes through them, entering the pharynx or throat. The air then moves through the oral or nasal section of the pharynx. The shape of the mouth or the nose modifies the moving air. Next, the air escapes from the nostrils or moves over the teeth, tongue, and lips (Figure 3.1). Depending on the position of these articulators, different sounds will result. In reality, the process is quite straightforward; the complex part of speech production is in the intricate *timing* involved in the physiological component of production. (See Appendix A for a reproduction of Figure 3.1 with blank lines in place of the labels.)

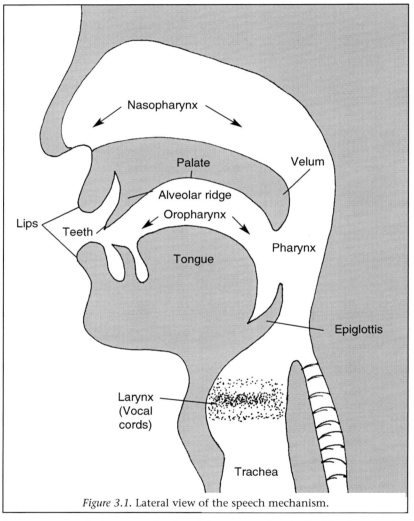

*Figure 3.1.* Lateral view of the speech mechanism.

## Physiology of Speech Production

The physiology of spoken language involves four activities: respiration, phonation, resonation, and articulation.

### Respiration

Respiration, or breathing, has both a primary and a secondary purpose. All humans breathe to maintain life—that is respiration's primary purpose. The secondary purpose is for speech. In either case, the individual must be able to control respiration in order to produce the desired effect. In producing a sound, air must be expelled from the lungs in an efficient and effective manner. Take a moment and yawn. Think about what is happening. Air is rushing from your lungs, traveling up the trachea, through the open vocal cords, and out of your mouth. Try to talk while yawning. It's not easy. Why? It is difficult to talk because the air is not exhaled as a controlled stream. You have to utilize the entire anatomical production system in order to produce speech on a yawn. This places a tremendous strain on the system.

In contrast, now take your time, inhale from the abdomen, and say the entire alphabet on a single exhaled breath stream. If you truly controlled your exhalation, you not only produced the entire alphabet but you also had breath to spare. The process of **controlled abdominal exhalation** is a critical first step to intelligible speech production. Without adequate breath support, you cannot produce an ongoing natural flow of speech.

Some individuals make the mistake of taking quick short breaths high up in the lungs. This is called clavicular breathing (breathing from the shoulders instead of the abdomen). It is inefficient for life support and especially for speech. Try the alphabet task again, this time taking only a short breath from your shoulders area. You undoubtedly had a much smaller quantity of air in your exhalation, became physically tense toward the end of the alphabet, and did not have any remaining air when you were finished. Imagine trying to talk on such a limited amount of air!

## Phonation

Phonation is a process that occurs when the vocal cords close and vibrate during exhalation. Another name for phonation is voicing. It is important to understand that not all speech sounds are voiced—only the sounds that are produced by vibrating vocal cords. For example, the *f* sound is a voiceless sound because there is no vocal cord vibration. Its counterpart, *v,* is voiced because of the vocal cord vibration. Try it.

Vocal cords in children, women, and men are physically different from one another. Men's vocal cords are longer in length and thicker in mass, thereby producing a lower vocal pitch. Generally speaking, women's vocal cords are not as long as men's and the mass of the cords is significantly less, producing a higher pitch. A child's vocal cords are even smaller with even less mass. The average vocal pitch for a child is around 250 Hz or middle C on a piano (Palmer, 1993).

One of the most amazing features of this part of the physiology of speech production is the timing that takes place between exhalation and the vibration of the vocal cords. In milliseconds, the air is exhaled; the vocal cords vibrate to produce a voiced sound, which then travels through the rest of the vocal tract to be modified and then appear as a speech sound. This respiration-phonation "ballet" is another essential component of intelligible speech production. Without the coordination of the two, speech production is impossible.

## Resonation

After the air moves through the vocal cords, it continues along a tube (the oropharynx and/or nasopharynx) and picks up characteristics of the tube. This is called resonance. Think about blowing air into the top of an empty bottle or running your finger around the edge of a crystal glass. You will hear different tones. The tones depend upon a number of the physical characteristics of sound as well as the size and shape of the bottle or glass. Your throat works the same way. Depending upon the mass and shape of your pharynx, the sound coming from the vocal cords will pick up different resonance characteristics. It is important because all of these sounds fall within various frequency ranges. We must be familiar with those frequencies so that we have a clear understanding of what our students with hearing loss will be able to hear and perceive acoustically when it comes to developing speech. After the sound resonates through the vocal tract, the articulators alter the sound and allow us to produce what is recognized as speech.

## Articulation

Articulation, the final step in the process, involves the use of the velum, palate, tongue, alveolar ridge, teeth, and lips to form what we know as vowels and consonants. It is the articulation process that gives humans the unique ability to produce speech.

In the course of articulating speech sounds, the velum or soft palate moves in a valvelike manner to open or block the entrance to the nasopharynx. (The nasopharynx is the portion of the throat that courses through the nasal cavity.) When the velum is up, sounds exit through the oral cavity. When the velum is down, sounds have a nasal quality because the air is moving both through the oral and nasal cavities.

As resonated air moves through the oral cavity, it passes over the tongue. The position of the tongue to some degree dictates the type of sound that will be produced. If the tongue is high and flat in the mouth near the palate, the air is constricted and squeezed through a space, giving it a turbulent characteristic. The *sh* sound is produced in this way. When the tongue is near the front of the mouth by the alveolar ridge, it may continue to provide a constricted air space, producing an *s* or *z* sound. The tongue is also the organ that is primarily responsible for the production of all vowel sounds. Other sounds are produced using the teeth and lips with or without movement by the tongue.

When discussing articulation, the term *Distinctive Feature* is often used to describe the speech sounds. These specific attributes, or distinctive features, of the articulation process are discussed later in the chapter in the section describing the segmental aspects of speech sounds.

## Reviewing Physiology of Speech Production

The production of a speech sound begins with exhalation of air from the lungs. The breath stream moves up through the trachea and vibrates the vocal folds, picks up pitch as it moves through the folds, and adds resonance as it travels through the vocal tract. The air exits the mouth or the nose after articulation by the velum, palate, tongue, alveolar ridge, teeth, and lips. Timing is critical in this process. An unsustained breath stream, problems in the vibration of the cords, resonance within the vocal tract, or miscues in articulation can all inhibit the development of intelligible speech production.

# The Relationship of Speech to the Five Components of Language

It is important to remember that speech is spoken language; although you can talk about the specific attributes of speech-sound production, you cannot divorce it from the other components of language. Speech, then, must be discussed from a language perspective. There are five major components of language: pragmatics, phonology, morphology, semantics, and syntax. Each component can be defined and discussed as a separate entity, but in reality, all five components continually interact with one another in coordination with the motor process of speech in order to produce spoken communication.

## Pragmatics and Discourse

Pragmatics and discourse are interwoven components of spoken communication. Pragmatics is a set of rules that governs the use of language in context (Nicolosi, Harriman, & Kresheck, 1996). A child learns how to use language differently depending on the context of the situation. Discourse is another name for conversation, or the exchange of ideas.

As human beings, we communicate because we want to. We have something to say and we want to share those thoughts and feelings with those around us. Babies communicate immediately with their parents or other significant caregivers. Through eye gazes, imitative cooing, repetitive babbling, and other forms of prelexical communication, babies are already participating in conversations (discourse, turn taking) and they quickly learn that they can get what they want (pragmatic function or intent) through those interactions.

Babies with hearing loss are no different. They also establish visual connectivity to their caretakers. Depending upon the type and degree of hearing loss, the child may also establish many of the oral linkages, too. It is well documented that deaf babies orally coo and babble on the same developmental schedule as hearing babies (Easterbrooks & Baker, 2002; Marschark, 1997). The breakdown in spoken communication begins when the parent discovers that a hearing loss is present. In many cases, the parents simply stop talking to the baby and the communication connection is completely severed.

## Phonology

Phonology involves the study of the way we use English sounds or phonemes in speech production. There are specific rules to be followed when words are produced in English; to break those rules causes the production of a word that is not identified as an English utterance. For example, it is perfectly acceptable in English to create words that begin with the *st* blend. *Stauforealeus* may not be a word that we know, but we are able to successfully and comfortably pronounce the word because it contains a phonological sequence that is acceptable in English. Consider *mxyzptlk!* How might you attack that word? It is not a typically acceptable combination of English phonemes and it takes more than a moment to determine how to say it: mixieplick, one of Superman's nemeses (Ordway & Janke, 1992).

Phonology encompasses the ability of an individual to motorically produce individual speech sounds and to use those sounds spontaneously in ongoing speech. Many teachers and speech therapists of D/HH children can attest to the fact that the children *can* articulate nearly all speech sounds when asked to do so in isolation, that is, say the sound all by itself or in a single word or simple phrase. But when the sounds are integrated into running conversation, they are often distorted at best or omitted entirely. Why does this happen? Daniel Ling (1989) discusses the concept of automaticity. **Automaticity** is the ability of an individual to use speech sounds without preplanning or self-monitoring production. In other words, you just say it and it comes out correctly. Ling believes strongly that a child will not develop spontaneous intelligible conversational skills until speech production reaches the level of automaticity.

***Phonemes: The Segmental Components of Speech.*** There are 43 phonemes in the English language. Phonemes may be classified according to their traits or characteristics. Typically, consonant phonemes are grouped according to their distinctive features of manner, place, and voicing. Table 3.1 (page 30) indicates the manner, place, and voicing for all the consonant sounds in English.

**Manner** refers to the way in which a sound is produced. Sounds such as /p/ and /b/, /t/ and /d/, or /k/ and /g/ that require a buildup of air pressure and then a quick release are called **plosive sounds.** Other sounds such as /s/, /z/, /f/, and /v/ require that air be constricted and slowly released. These are called **fricative sounds.**

**Place** refers to the location along the vocal tract where the sounds are produced. Sounds that are made at the lips are called **bilabials** (e.g., /p/, /b/, /m/); those made in the back of the throat are called **lingua-velar** (e.g., /k/, /g/).

**Voicing** refers to vibration of the vocal cords during sound production. If the vocal cords vibrate, the sounds are voiced (e.g., /d/, /z/, /n/). If the cords do not vibrate, the sounds are voiceless (e.g., /t/, /s/, /h/).

*Vowels.* English vowels are classified in a different way. Vowels are described by the placement of the tongue within the oral cavity. If you think of the inside of your mouth as a flat-bottomed triangle, the tongue moves back and forth and up and down within the triangle. The difference in position accounts for the different vowels. See Figure 3.2 (page 31) for illustrations of the relationship between position and vowel sound.

Vowels are also described by their **formants**. Formants are defined as a "frequency

| | *Table 3.1.* **Distinctive features of English consonants.** | | |
|---|---|---|---|
| **Consonant sound** | **Manner** | **Place** | **Voicing** |
| p | stop-plosive | bilabial | voiceless |
| b | stop-plosive | bilabial | voiced |
| t | stop-plosive | lingua-alveolar | voiceless |
| d | stop-plosive | lingua-alveolar | voiced |
| k | stop-plosive | lingua-velar | voiceless |
| g | stop-plosive | lingua-velar | voiced |
| th[1] | fricative | lingua-dental | voiceless |
| th[2] | fricative | lingua-dental | voiced |
| f | fricative | labio-dental | voiceless |
| v | fricative | labio-dental | voiced |
| s | fricative | lingua-alveolar | voiceless |
| z | fricative | lingua-alveolar | voiced |
| sh | fricative | lingua-palatal | voiceless |
| zh | fricative | lingua-palatal | voiced |
| wh | fricative | bilabial | voiceless |
| h | fricative | glottal | voiceless |
| ch | affricate | lingua-alveolar-palatal | voiceless |
| j | affricate | lingua-alveolar-palatal | voiced |
| qu | affricate | bilabial-lingua-velar | voiceless |
| x | affricate | lingua-velar-alveolar | voiceless |
| m | nasal | bilabial | voiced |
| n | nasal | lingua-alveolar | voiced |
| ng | nasal | lingua-velar | voiced |
| l | lateral/liquid | lingua-alveolar | voiced |
| r | lateral | lingua-palatal | voiced |
| y | semivowel | lingua-palatal | voiced |
| w | semivowel | bilabial | voiced |

region, for vowels and resonant consonants, in which a relatively high degree of acoustic energy is concentrated" (Nicolosi et al., 1996, p. 116). Formants are like bands of sound energy that are concentrated, occur across time, and distinguish one vowel from another. Every vowel has a series of formants that are related to the resonance characteristics of that vowel. Formants are typically labeled $F_1$, $F_2$, and so forth. The $F_1$ formant is essentially the same for all vowels. It occurs in the low Hertz range (250–500 Hz). It is when you get to the higher formants that an individual's auditory perception skills have an impact on his ability to discriminate between vowel sounds.

To help clarify the concept of formants, consider that your mouth is like a bottle, open at one end (your lips) and closed at the other (vocal cords). When sound is introduced in the bottle (vocal cords vibrate sending a sound into your oral cavity), the sound can appear to be high in pitch, low in pitch, or anywhere in between; it all depends on the length and mass of your vocal cords and how the sound is resonating through the space. If you change the inside shape of the bottle, you change the way the sound vibrates and can then produce specific tones. That is how vowel production

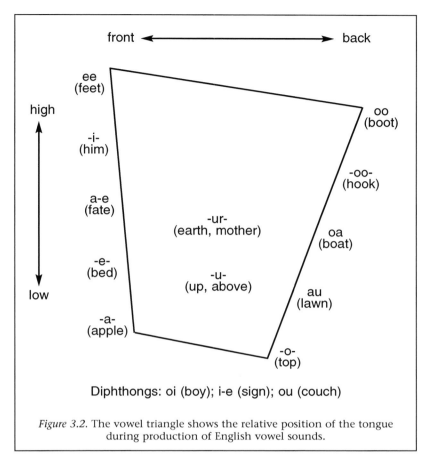

front ◄──────────► back

high

ee
(feet)

-i-
(him)

a-e
(fate)

-e-
(bed)

low

-a-
(apple)

-ur-
(earth, mother)

-u-
(up, above)

oo
(boot)

-oo-
(hook)

oa
(boat)

au
(lawn)

-o-
(top)

Diphthongs: oi (boy); i-e (sign); ou (couch)

*Figure 3.2.* The vowel triangle shows the relative position of the tongue during production of English vowel sounds.

works. If you open your mouth slightly and say "ah," your tongue is low and flat, making your oral cavity wide open; the resonant sound that is produced is "ah." If you change your tongue position, move it forward and high (close to your front teeth), the vowel will change to "ee." You have changed the shape inside the bottle, and the way the sound resonates (the formants that are created) through the bottle produces a different vowel sound.

It is important to recognize the various features of consonant and vowel speech sounds because there is a direct relationship between the sound output and a child's ability to auditorally perceive both environmental and speech sounds. Figure 3.3 (page 32) shows the relationship between speech and environmental sounds plotted on an audiogram. Fricative sounds are typically high frequency sounds, those that are above 2000 Hz. The second, third, and fourth formants of vowels are also above 1000 Hz. Children who have hearing above 1000 Hz can perceive many of the high frequency sounds, vowel formants, and consonant-vowel transitions—a critical insight for the speech facilitator when helping to develop or enhance speech production.

***Suprasegmental Components of Speech.*** The inaccurate articulation of consonants and vowels is only one reason why speech may be unintelligible. In addition, several other components of speech provide flavor to the mix. These components are called the suprasegmental or prosodic aspects of speech. They include intensity (stress and inflection), duration (rate and phrasing), and intonation (pitch). The suprasegmental aspects add rhythm and tone to speech production.

**Intensity** refers to the emphasis placed on a word in a sentence. An emphasized word is slightly louder. Consider the question, "What did you do?" How many different meanings might this single utterance convey? Examine the variations in intensity on the meanings below:

| | |
|---|---|
| **WHAT** did you do? | *Surprise, incredulous inquiry* |
| What **DID** you do? | *Disbelief, blaming* |
| What did **YOU** do? | *Accusatory* |
| What did you **DO**? | *Furtive inquiry, concern* |

Clearly, the meaning behind each of these questions changed even though the words in the question remained the same. The suprasegmental component of intensity or stress affected speech production and the ultimate meaning of the message.

**Duration** refers to the length of a sound, word, or phrase. When you change duration, you decrease or increase the rate of speech production and therefore change the rhythm of the message. Rhythm and rate are two components of duration. Rhythm is made up of intensity and duration characteristics. Rhythm includes stress within word production as well as inflection or phrasing within the entire utterance. Rate relates to the speed with which a speaker articulates. If a speaker has difficulty in the rhythm or rate aspects of speech, even though all sounds may be articulated perfectly, speech will be hard to understand. The following example will help to highlight this point. What is this person trying to say?

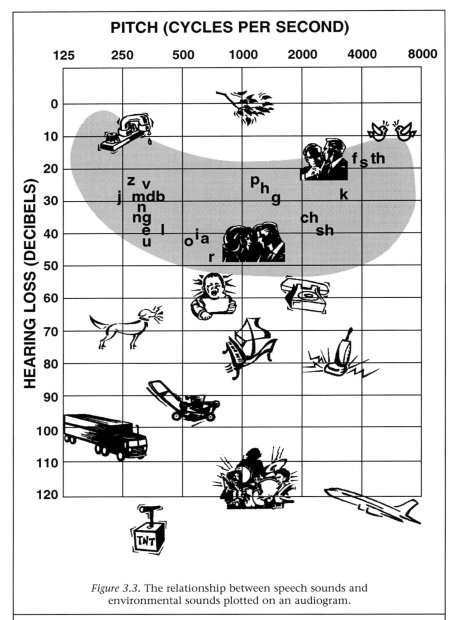

*Figure 3.3.* The relationship between speech sounds and environmental sounds plotted on an audiogram.

*Note:* From *Hearing in Children*, 5th Edition (p. 18), by J. L. Northern and M. P. Downs, 2002, Baltimore: Lippincott Williams & Wilkins. Copyright 2002 by Lippincott Williams & Wilkins. Reprinted with permission.

WhatamIbidwhatamIbidwhatamIbidbidadollarbidadollar
Bidadollarbidadollarbidtwobidtwobidtwobidfivebidfivebidfive
whatamIbidwhatamIbidwhatamIbid?

The cadence of a professional auctioneer makes understanding the auctioneer's speech difficult because of the speed and the lack of breaks in the flow of the utterance. Auctioneers articulate every sound in these words, but the speed of production makes it sound garbled!

Errors in rhythm and rate occur on the opposite end as well. What would speech sound like if every syllable had equal stress and inflection? It would sound robotic, monotonic, and boring. It would also be difficult to understand. A listener would quickly lose interest in the communicative efforts made by this type of speaker. Again, although articulation might be precise and perfect, a significant communication breakdown would occur.

**Intonation** refers to the rise and fall of the voice to enhance the meaning of a spoken communication. The meaning of what is being said is often carried in the melodic pitch of the utterance and accompanies the facial expression of the speaker. Comedians often use a change in intonation in presenting their jokes. Think of your favorite comedian. The intonation that accompanies the joke can bring an audience to tears, not only because of the scenario in which it is spoken, but because the purposeful use of pitch supports the comedic message. Different intonation would not have the same effect and would, in essence, change the meaning of the utterance, ruining the joke. Sarcasm is another form of exchange that is effective because of the user's intonation.

***Some Common Suprasegmental Errors.*** Parents, teachers, and SLPs who work in formal situations with deaf and hard of hearing children often promote erroneous production of suprasegmentals. Parents want their child to be understood and may demand that articulation be precise. That is a major error made by parents; by insisting that a child articulate every single speech sound accurately, the natural rhythm (coarticulation) within words breaks down. The child will sound robotic or mechanical in his speech production.

Teachers mistakenly guide students into producing speech that has equal stress on all syllables. This is done in a variety of ways, but the two most common occur when the teacher is teaching a new multisyllabic word. Instead of modeling the word using the natural rhythm and inflection, the word is broken into discrete syllables, sometimes into discrete phonemes, and the child is asked to repeat the word that way, rather than the correctly coarticulated way. The result is a word that has hyper-accurate articulation and syllabication, but is far removed from the correctly coarticulated production.

The second error frequently made by teachers is the exaggerated reduction of the rate of speech when communicating with the children. Far too often, teachers become monotonic and slow in their rate of speech during instruction. The model presented to the child is one of reduced rate and inaccurate rhythm and inflection. Children will reproduce what they hear. If the teacher is presenting an impoverished spoken communication environment, the student will follow with a similar level of production.

Speech and language pathologists make many of the same errors as teachers and parents. Attempts to make speech accurate rather than intelligible cause therapists to focus for unnecessarily long periods of time on phonetic production of sounds. There is a relatively small amount of time spent on phonological use of speech sounds. Suprasegmentals are all but ignored. It is no wonder then that a child can produce a sound perfectly when working with the speech therapist or teacher, but once he gets onto the playground, it's as if he never produced the sound at all!

# Morphology

Morphology may be defined as the smallest word or part of a word that has meaning. In English there are free and bound morphemes. Free morphemes can stand alone and carry meaning all by themselves (e.g., *chair* or *woof*). Bound morphemes must be attached to another word to carry meaning (e.g., *s* or *ing* or *pre*). These are critical components of spoken communication because they carry a great deal of meaning. Free morphemes are what we typically think of as vocabulary words. Bound morphemes are lexical markers for tense, number (plurals), possession, and so forth.

Unfortunately, in English, the bound markers are often unstressed during normal speech production and they are also often high frequency sounds. This combination has a significant impact on a child's ability to perceive speech. A child with a high frequency hearing loss will have difficulty perceiving the bound morphemes, which will impact his understanding of a linguistic message. A child who cannot hear an *s* or *z* at the end of a word may have a hard time recognizing that a word is supposed to be plural. The same can be said for past tense words that end in the /t/ sound (e.g., *walked, laughed*). The child will be unable to hear the /t/ sound and therefore will not recognize that the statement had a past tense meaning. Ling (1989) notes that with proper amplification and appropriately fitted earmolds, this should not be an issue for many children with hearing loss.

## Semantics

The classic definition of semantics is "the meaning of language," and when we think of semantics, we typically think of the vocabulary words that make up our language. But semantics involves much more than vocabulary words. Semantics includes figurative use of words, multiple word meanings, the use of "function" words, and the many colorful ways in which language can be expressed.

Where does spoken communication fit into this picture? One of the major difficulties a child with hearing loss has is the ability to learn new words in a spontaneous and natural way. If a child does not have the vocabulary needed to successfully share a thought, feeling, or need, communication will clearly be affected. Unfortunately, many of the most commonly used speech sounds are those that are the last to develop in normally hearing children. The /s/, /z/, and /l/ sounds (among others) are difficult to produce and frequently used in English. In addition, many of those sounds are high frequency sounds, not easily heard by a child with a severe to profound hearing loss.

The best way to help a child with hearing loss to develop good semantic skills is through dialogue and discourse; in other words, *conversation.* Just as the use of single sound practice does little to assist in the phonological use of speech sounds, individual word practice does little to enhance the semantics skills of deaf and hard of hearing children. The ability to use speech sounds semantically depends upon the child's exposure to those sounds on a regular and correctly modeled basis in language-rich contexts.

## Syntax

Syntax, or grammar, involves the rules that govern the word order used to express a thought. We follow a series of rules that allow us to create an infinite number of sentences. If we fail to follow the appropriate rules, then our communicative efforts don't make sense. A child who has a hearing loss may have difficulty with the syntactical aspects of spoken language. Difficulties occur not only because the child does not hear and have the opportunity to assimilate the rules of spoken English automatically but also because so much meaning is carried through the word order and suprasegmental components of speech. As demonstrated previously in this chapter, any difficulty perceiving those suprasegmental aspects of speech will have a direct impact on the understanding and use of basic English syntax.

# Final Thoughts

Speech production is a complicated process that is acquired by hearing children in an amazingly natural way. Hearing loss and speech production are not mutually exclusive. Hearing loss can have a major impact on a child's ability to understand and produce speech, but hearing loss in and of itself does not eliminate a child's potential to develop intelligible spoken language skills. With early intervention, amplification, and regular high-quality interactions with people at home and school, a child who has a profound hearing loss *can* potentially develop excellent speech skills.

# Summary

In this chapter, we reviewed the anatomy and physiology of the speech mechanism. The speech production sequence from respiration to articulation was examined. We noted that speech is a component of language and that one cannot talk about speech or spoken communication without examining it from a linguistic perspective. Hearing loss has an impact on all aspects of language. We also discussed a number of important speech characteristics: distinctive features, formants, and prosody. A child's speech intelligibility depends not only on the accuracy of his articulation, but the appropriate utilization of the suprasegmental components of spoken communication. We noted some of the well-meaning, but erroneous strategies that parents, teachers, and SLPs often use in their efforts to help a deaf or hard of hearing child improve his speech production. Finally, we discussed the importance of morphology, semantics, and syntax in helping D/HH children attain fluency in spoken communication.

# Chapter 3 Topics for Discussion

1. Describe each of the five components of language from a spoken communication perspective.

2. Explain the importance of understanding the relationship of formants to speech perception and production.

3. Listen to a recorded speech production sample and describe the speech characteristics on the basis of suprasegmental production.

4. Explain the physiological processes that make up the act of speech production.

*Chapter 4*

# Amplification and Cochlear Implants

There are many different types of amplification systems. From a personally designed hearing aid or cochlear implant to sound-field amplification, some form of assistive listening device is available to help nearly every person with a hearing loss. This chapter will describe the various types of systems and provide the reader with resources for more information regarding each system.

## How Does a Hearing Aid Work?

Dillon (2001) describes hearing aids as "basically a miniature public-address system" (p.10). This is an excellent analogy. If you consider the intent of a hearing aid—to make available sound louder and if possible clearer to the listener—then a hearing aid does indeed serve the function of a public address system!

A hearing aid is designed to pick up an acoustic signal (sounds, speech) through a microphone. The microphone is typically directional, which means it can pick up sounds from any direction but has a stronger sensitivity toward the front of the head and will pick up sounds that come from the front of the listener better than those that come from the back. The purpose of the microphone is to change or transduce the acoustic (sound) energy into electrical energy. This is why a microphone is also referred to as a transducer. The change takes place internally in the microphone. After the sound is transduced into electrical energy, it moves into a tiny amplifier whose job is to make the entering sound larger. The amplifier gets its power from the hearing aid battery. Sound can be amplified in many different ways; the type and degree of hearing loss will dictate the best kind of amplifier for an aid. After the sound is amplified and modified as needed, it then moves on to a receiver. The receiver converts the modified electrical signal back into an acoustic output signal (sound). That sound signal is sent to the earmold and into the listener's ear.  When one considers the incredibly small size of many personal hearing aids today, it is truly wondrous that this piece of equipment can do so much!

With today's technology, hearing aids can be designed to significantly reduce the amount of background noise (nonspeech sounds) that is processed by the hearing aid. They can be designed to specifically enhance the amplification of certain sounds or ranges of frequencies (pitches). Aids can be designed to reduce sound clutter or noise. The one thing an aid cannot do is replace sounds that are not already available to the person who has a hearing loss. In other words, to be able to have a sound modified for you to be able to hear it, your cochlea must have some capacity to hear that sound. If the type and degree of hearing loss precludes the ability to hear particular sounds, a hearing aid will not be able to replace those sounds.

# Types of Personal Hearing Aids

The first hearing aids were described and used in the 1600s. The trumpet, horn, funnel, and speaking tube were all means of modifying the acoustic environment to create a louder sound. The first wearable model of a hearing aid that had a microphone, battery, amplifier, and receiver was made in 1902. It was called the Akouphone and the Acousticon (Dillon, 2001).

## Body Aids

Traditionally, body style aids were the first aids worn by children. They were considered more durable and more powerful than ear-level aids. Body aids look like a rectangular box that is worn in a harness or carrier pouch on the child's chest. The microphone is in the box and the transduced sound is sent along cords to a button-style receiver that is attached to the earmold. The earmold directs the amplified sound into the ear. Protective covers were made to help keep the body aid free of food debris and liquids.

## Ear-Level Aids

Technology today is such that infants often receive ear-level hearing aids as the first hearing aid. There are a number of kinds of ear-level hearing aids.

*Behind-the-Ear Aids.* The most commonly used aid for children is the **behind-the-ear (BTE) hearing aid.** This is a two-piece hearing aid with an arc-shaped plastic case that contains the microphone and all of the other electronic equipment that converts and boosts the incoming sound. This component sits behind the ear. The earmold is connected to the BTE with a small piece of plastic tubing that fits over the top of the ear. The sound travels through the tubing into the ear through the earmold.

*In-the-Ear Aids.* Three other ear-level hearing aids are available but not typically used with children. These included the in-the-ear (ITE), in-the-canal (ITC), and the completely-in-the-canal (CIC) hearing aids. As their names indicate, these hearing aids are much smaller; the entire aid fits in the ear canal, with no parts outside the physical structure of the ear. All of the components fit into one compact case. Adults typically prefer these aids for cosmetic purposes. Because these aids are tiny and can be difficult to remove, they are not practical for use with children.

***Analog and Digital Hearing Aids.*** Hearing aids are produced using two different types of technology. The traditional form of amplification technology is the use of **analog technology.** In this form of amplification, the acoustic sound pressure is analogous to the electric current or voltage being produced in the aid. When the pressure of an acoustic signal increases, so does the voltage required to produce that signal. Analog technology is less precise and is more likely to allow for various types of sound distortion to occur in the amplified sound that is transmitted to the ear.

The latest amplification technology involves the use of **digital signals**. A special converter in the hearing aid is used to change the analog electrical signal into a series of number strings. Digital signals are comprised of a combination of 1s and 0s. Sounds are mathematically converted to these numerical signals, and no information regarding the sound is lost. This makes digital technology far superior to analog because the information regarding the sound is accurate.

Digital hearing aids became available in the 1990s. Currently, the greatest drawback to owning a digital aid is the high cost. As with other forms of technology, continued development will allow the price of digital aids to come down, making them more accessible and ultimately the hearing aid of choice for all users in the future.

***Other Aids.*** Two additional types of hearing aids are available, although neither is used with great frequency. The eyeglass or spectacle hearing aid is worn with prescription eyeglasses. The arm piece of the glasses, which fits over the ear, is adapted to allow for the wearer to use a BTE hearing aid. The other type of aid is a bone-conduction hearing aid. The bone-conduction hearing aid is used when there is no ear canal present, for example, in the case of congenital atresia. This type of aid has no earmold; instead it is worn with some form of headband or headpiece that allows an amplifier (bone oscillator) in a small plastic case to sit on the mastoid bone. The bone oscillator then transmits the sound through the mastoid bone directly to the cochlea.

## Ling 5 or 6 Sound Test

Until a child is old enough to be responsible for her own hearing aid maintenance, it is important for all members of the team to be familiar with the procedures used for checking the hearing system for proper functioning. The parents, teacher, or speech and language pathologist should have a special stethoscope that couples with a BTE-style hearing aid. Through visual inspection and by using the stethoscope, the listener can complete the following maintenance activities:

- the battery is functioning properly; sound is not intermittent but steady
- the gain wheel is working smoothly and there are no jumps or drops in volume
- there are no blockages in the earmold or cracks in the tubing
- each switch is moving and functioning properly
- the sound produced by the aid is distortion-free

In order to complete this last task, the listener should perform the Ling 5 or 6 Sound Test (Ling, 1989). This test enables the listener to determine if essential acoustic components are working correctly in the hearing aid and if the child is able to use the aid to receive those sounds. The 5 or 6 Sound Test was designed to assess the individual's ability to receive the important acoustic features of speech sounds across the speech frequency spectrum (250–8,000 Hz). The test incorporates the reception of first and second formants, and the fricative turbulence of high frequency speech sounds. The listener should first do the test while listening to the aid through the stethoscope, and then repeat the test with the child while she is wearing the hearing aid.

While listening through the stethoscope, say the following sounds in the order given, one at a time:

oo———aw————ee———sh———s

Listen for distortion. If the sounds are not being produced accurately through the hearing aid, it is in need of repair. A hearing aid that provides a distorted signal to a child is of absolutely no benefit.

Next, if the aid sounds good to you, have the child put on the aid and stand about two yards from you. Ask the child to close her eyes and clap when she hears each of the five sounds. Again, say each sound, one at a time at a normal loudness, and give the child time to clap. If the child responds to each sound with a clap, then you can be reasonably sure that she is detecting the sounds.

Finally, ask the child to close her eyes and repeat the five sounds after you say each of them. If the child is successful in her attempts, then you can be reasonably sure that she is able to identify the sounds being heard.

In some cases, the teacher may want to use a sixth sound, /m/. If the student is not responding to the vowel sounds, the teacher will want to see if she responds to the lone production of /m/. The /m/ sound is very low frequency. If the student does not respond to /m/, this is a clear indication that there is some major problem occurring either with the hearing aid or the child's physical hearing ability.

It is important to do this test every day because it quickly indicates the integrity of the hearing aid and the child's ability to use the aid to receive important acoustic information. The following website contains more information on the Ling 5 or 6 Sound Test:

■   www.hardofhearingchildren.com/Great%Information/ling_sound_test.htm

# Group/Remote Amplification Systems

In addition to a personal hearing aid, there are systems that allow an individual to receive amplified sound in the general environment. Each of these systems is set up to accommodate a listener's needs in a large group setting. Typically, sound engineers examine the acoustic properties of a facility to determine what the best system would be for that particular environment. Educational audiologists examine classroom environments and other school environments to determine the best sound input combinations for a child with hearing loss.

### Induction Loop System
The **induction loop system** uses the connection between electricity and magnetism to enable sound to be transmitted to a telecoil inside a personal hearing aid. An induction loop is a hardwire system that can be set up in a large area, such as around the periphery of a room, or in a small personal area, such as surrounding a favorite chair. The sound waves within the loop area are converted into electrical current that flows through the wire and into a magnetic field, which is then picked up by the telecoil wire inside the hearing aid. The voltage is amplified and converted back to sound by a receiver. That sound is transmitted to the listener through the T or telecoil setting of the hearing aid. This system provides a better signal-to-noise ratio for the listener. The signal received through

the telecoil sounds as if the speaker is closer to the person wearing the hearing aid than if the microphone were used alone. Induction loops can be set up in classrooms or anywhere in a home environment. The major disadvantage of a loop system is that the listener must be within the loop system environment to receive the signal.

## Frequency Modulated Systems

**FM (Frequency Modulated) Systems** are a second type of group system; they use radio-frequency transmissions. This is a portable system that allows the user to move among many different environments and maintain an excellent signal-to-noise ratio (SNR) with little distortion. The speaker wears a transmitter that sends the speech signal at a particular FM frequency. The listener wears a receiver that is either a separate listening device or a device coupled to the personal hearing aid. The receiver is set to match the FM frequency of the transmitter. In this way, multiple FM units can be used within the same environment, but each listener receives only the information sent by his or her specific FM transmitter. These systems can be used in virtually any environment, from a classroom in a school for deaf children to a classroom in a neighborhood school to an area completely separate from the school such as a field trip to the zoo.

The FM systems differ from loop systems in that they *do not* convert sound to another form of energy. Instead, the transmitter modulates (modifies) the sound (carrier) signal, and a receiver picks up the modulated signal and produces a voltage that is proportional to the original signal. There are two major disadvantages to FM transmission systems. The range of FM signals available for transmission is dictated by regulatory agencies. Each country has specified bands that are licensed to be available for FM uses. Also, on occasion, an FM user may experience an interfering signal or dropout (the signal is lost).

## Infrared System

A third form of group amplification is **infrared transmission.** Infrared works on the principles of electromagnetic radio energy but at a much higher frequency. This is an electromagnetic signal that is perceived as red light. This signal behaves like light waves, so it can be easily blocked or attenuated (reduced) by items in the environment. The audio signal is modulated as an infrared light signal; the receiver picks up the infrared signal using a headphone, earphone, or coupling device attached to the personal hearing aid, and converts the light signal back to an audio signal. This type of device is often used in public auditoriums and theaters. Infrared transmitters are placed strategically throughout the room, and the listener wears a headphone device that allows reception of the performance.

## Sound-Field System

A final system that is gaining popularity is the **classroom sound-field amplification system.** The amplification system is based on the use of acoustic gain in the environment; the listener receives acoustic signals through the regular microphone of the personal hearing aid. This system is based on the premise that a general increase in the intensity of the speech signal in the open environment reduces the level of the background sound enhancing the signal-to-noise ratio (SNR). This is accomplished by placing speakers strategically around the classroom. The teacher speaks into a microphone and the message is amplified for everyone in the class. The system can be limiting to the teacher's ability to move around the classroom because of the wires connected to the microphone. This can be remedied by using an FM link between the teacher and the amplifier, which then allows the teacher to move effortlessly around the room.

## Reviewing Group/Remote Amplification Systems

Each of these systems has strengths as well as disadvantages (Table 4.1). The major strength of the FM, loop, and infrared systems is the significant increase in the SNR because the sound is transmitted in a nonacoustic form. There is much less opportunity for distortion and reverberation in the signal. The sound-field amplification system is the most convenient and least expensive. In addition, it has the potential to help *all* of the students in the classroom maintain their focus on the instruction, and it can help reduce vocal strain for the teacher. Major disadvantages, in general, include the drop and interference problems experienced by FM systems, transmission blockage for infrared systems, the limiting spatial nature of the loop systems, and the possibility of less than adequate SNR increases in the sound-field amplification systems.

### Table 4.1.
### Advantages and disadvantages of group/remote amplification systems.

| System | Advantages | Disadvantages |
|---|---|---|
| Induction loop | Good signal-noise ratio<br>Less reverberation<br>Consistent and reliable<br>Generally interference free<br>Low cost | Least convenient to use<br>Teacher stays within a designated space<br>Hearing aid must be in the "T" position |
| Frequency modulated | Good signal-noise ratio<br>No reverberation<br>Convenient | Less consistent because of "dropout" and outside interference<br>Several receivers and transmitters, batteries and charging units<br>Can be expensive |
| Infrared | Good signal-noise ratio<br>Less reverberation<br>Convenient<br>Good for large spaces<br>No spillover<br>Private | Occasional dropouts if transmitter does not face listener<br>Signal acts like light waves and can be blocked or accidentally bounced off another surface |
| Sound-field | Good signal-noise ratio<br>Less reverberation<br>Convenient<br>Consistent and reliable<br>No special equipment required<br>Low cost | Can lose S-N ratio benefit if room noise increases<br>Can have only one person speak at a time unless you have multiple microphones<br>Can get reverberation from poorly placed speakers |

# Cochlear Implants

"Cochlear implants are biomedical electronic devices that convert sound into electrical current to stimulate remaining auditory nerve elements directly, thereby producing hearing sensations" (Beiter & Brimacombe, 2000, p. 473). Cochlear implants *do not* restore normal hearing.

## How a Cochlear Implant Works

The cochlear implant is composed of a microphone, a speech processor, a transmitter and receiver/ stimulator, and electrodes. The internal parts of the implant are the receiver/stimulator and the electrode array. The receiver/stimulator is surgically embedded into the mastoid/occipital bones of the skull. These bones are behind and slightly above the top of the ear. This component includes an antenna and miniaturized electronics and is housed in a hermetically sealed plastic unit. The electrode array is a series of tiny electrodes (from 8–22 electrodes) on an inch-long fine wire that is inserted into the cochlea. The external parts of the implant include the microphone, which is worn like a traditional BTE hearing aid, the speech processor, and the transmitter. The speech processor with a battery looks similar to a body-type hearing aid and is worn in a shirt pocket, attached to a belt loop, or kept in some sort of comfortable carrier. The transmitter is a small plastic ring that sits on the scalp behind the ear. It is magnetically attached to the receiver that is embedded beneath the skin on the skull.

## Types of Cochlear Implants

There are currently three cochlear implant systems that have United States Food and Drug Administration (FDA) approval: the Cochlear Corporation Nucleus 22 and Nucleus 24 models and the Clarion Multi-Strategy Cochlear Implant System. The primary difference in the systems is the way in which speech is processed by the speech processor. All systems, however, follow the same general principles in how sound is transmitted to the cochlea. The directional microphone picks up sound, converts it to electrical energy, and sends it through a cord to the speech processor. The speech processor takes the electrical energy and digitizes it based upon the specific system integral to that processor. The digitized sound then goes back up the cord to the transmitter, which sends the sound transdermally (through the skin) to the receiver in the skull. The receiver then converts the digitized signals to electrical energy that is sent to the electrode array. The electrodes are pro-grammed to respond to specific ranges of electrical energy. When an electrode is stimulated, it in turn stimulates the corresponding area in the cochlea (the low pitches are at the far [apical] end of the cochlea and the high pitches are closest to the base of the cochlea). The nerve fibers that are stimulated then send the electrical impulse through the auditory nerve to the brain and the brain perceives sound.

It is important to understand that not every individual can benefit from a cochlear implant. They are designed for persons who are profoundly deaf and do not have useable residual hearing. Hearing aids are of no benefit to these individuals. The anatomy of the cochlea must be compatible for the electrode array. There are cases where infection or trauma causes anatomical distortions that would have a negative impact on the placement or function of the electrode array.

In the case of pediatric candidates, implantation under the age of two years is not yet consistently recommended. A trial period of hearing aid use is suggested to allow the child the opportunity to develop basic auditory reception skills and beginning language skills. If a child shows no increased auditory or linguistic abilities after the trial period, then implantation may be considered. With a very young child, the parents make the decision. In an older child or adolescent, it is critical that her own feelings, perceptions, and expectations are considered. Children whose parents force consideration of cochlear implantation do not make good candidates for the surgery.

It is essential that the family understand the commitment required for the cochlear implant process, beginning with surgery and following through with comprehensive long-term habilitation services. Recent research indicates that the highly successful pediatric candidate will be able to use the implant to develop fine-tuned auditory reception skills, speech perception skills, and receptive/expressive oral language skills. In addition, she will be able to adjust to newer implant technologies as they become available, to continue her development of enhanced auditory skills.

# Summary

In summary, the amplification systems available today are varied and offer multiple opportunities for enhancing hearing abilities. Personal hearing aids continue to advance technologically and are now fully programmable to meet the specific needs of the wearer. In addition, digital technology enables sound to be produced with quality precision and considerably reduced distortion. The cost of digital hearing aids will fall over time, making them more accessible to the vast majority of hearing aid users. Group/remote amplification devices also continue to show advancement and enable people in a wide-open environment to receive amplified signals with improved signal-to-noise ratios, less distortion, and more flexibility. Finally, cochlear implants continue to provide startling new advances in a deaf individual's ability to perceive and use speech sounds. The future is bright for an individual's continued development of the auditory sensory channel.

# Chapter 4 Topics for Discussion

1. Identify the six types of hearing aids described in this chapter and graph the strong and weak points for each.

2. Explain in layman's terms the purpose for amplification and how a hearing aid works.

3. What is the purpose for group amplification devices?

4. Calvin and Sheryl are attending a lecture at the local library and plan to make use of assistive listening devices. What type of device is likely to be available in the library lecture hall? Why is that the likely system?

5. Kelley is in fifth grade at her local school and is in need of a schoolwide assistive listening device. What type of device would be best for her? Why?

6. Cochlear implants have proponents and opponents with strong opinions regarding their use. Choose one side of the argument and support your contentions.

# *Part II*

# Applications

# Introduction to Part II

Now that the reader is more comfortable with the foundations of spoken communication, we can turn our focus to applying this knowledge in the classroom.

# Dispelling Myths and Misconceptions

The relationship between speech potential and deaf education has long been fraught with controversy. Experts have given their opinions over the years, and we, too, tend to encourage others to "see things our way." Most professionals and others who share their opinions are well intended. But without the full picture, parents may be forced to go the way of the professional with the best sales pitch, rather than getting all of the information and then seeking the decision that best meets their individual child's needs. The following is a list of common misconceptions that have permeated the area of deaf education for decades.

- **Speech equals intelligence.** Whether intentional or unintentional, many people equate a student's ability to speak with his level of intelligence. The truth is, there is no correlation between intelligible speech and intelligence level.
- **Signers cannot be speakers.** Some people believe that if you learn sign language, you will not develop spoken communication skills. The truth is, students who use sign language have the same spoken communication capabilities as those who do not.
- **Auditory/Oral students always have intelligible speech.** The truth is, students in Auditory/Oral classrooms have more exposure to spoken English, but this is no guarantee that they will all develop intelligible speech.

- **Predictions about a student's potential for spoken communication can be made based on his audiogram.** The truth is, you can never make predictions on speech intelligibility using any single device, and certainly not on one audiogram.
- **The more time spent in drill and tutoring, the better the child's speech will become.** The truth is, some students make great progress with little or no private tutoring. Others with many hours invested in tutoring still struggle to have intelligible speech.

Spoken communication may be seen as a continuum with "no spoken communication skills" on one end and "completely intelligible speech" on the other end.

If we begin to think in terms of progress along a continuum and *not* striving for perfection, then all students will meet with success.

# An Effective Speech Program

In order to set up an effective speech program, four components are necessary:
1. Supportive team
2. Positive classroom environment
3. Working evaluation
4. Proven teaching strategies

## Supportive Team
As noted in Chapter 1, a multidisciplinary team that works collaboratively toward the needs of the student can and will make all the difference in terms of a student's potential communicative success. But just having a close-knit team is not enough to facilitate success.

## Positive Classroom Environment
The student must feel safe and secure in the instructional environment. If we want students to communicate, the classroom needs to be speech-friendly in a number of ways. The classroom setting and the structure of the multidisciplinary team depend upon where the student receives his educational services in accordance with the IEP.

The student who attends a magnet school for deaf children will have a different type of team and setting than the child who attends his neighborhood school and sees his deaf education teacher for academic support once a week. It is important to be aware of the various service delivery models available for deaf and hard of hearing children today. It is not the intent to discuss the advantages or disadvantages of these options, but rather to provide a brief description of each. Stewart and Kluwin (2001) provide an excellent description of the various educational settings. We are summarizing their information in the following section.

## Service Delivery Models

*Self-Contained Classroom.* The self-contained classroom is traditionally found in residential or day schools for deaf children. In the self-contained class, all of the students in the class are homogeneous with regard to their age or grade level, and their IEPs indicate that it is least restrictive for them to be in an environment where all of the students are deaf. On occasion one might find a self-contained class for deaf children in a regular public school. In that case, it is likely that the children in the class will have mixed age and grade ranges, in addition to the normal ranges of ability and modes of communication used, but, again, their IEPs will have dictated that a self-contained environment was the one least restrictive for the child.

*Resource Room.* This teaching assignment finds the teacher in a variety of settings in the school, from a converted closet to a nice-sized classroom. The resource room teacher may work with a single child or a small group of children at one time. The deaf and hard of hearing students typically do not have their home-base with the deaf education teacher, but are primarily in classrooms with their hearing peers. The D/HH students come to the resource room only for specific instructional periods or activities. Resource rooms can be found at any grade level and are common at the high school level when there are a relatively large number of students with hearing loss.

*Co-Enrollment Classroom.* This is a relatively new model of delivering services to deaf and hard of hearing students. In this case, the ratio of D/HH students to hearing students is 1:2. There are two teachers, one certified as a general education teacher and the other as a deaf education teacher. The two teachers share all teaching responsibilities for all subjects, plan their instructional activities together, and collaborate closely in meeting the needs of all students in the class. The general education teacher becomes more familiar with and in some cases extremely fluent in the use of sign language. The deaf education teacher, in addition to his expertise in sign language, is primarily responsible for implementing the specially designed instruction noted in the IEPs.

*Itinerant.* The itinerant teacher is now the most common type of teacher found in deaf education. There has been a significant shift in student educational placement in the last thirty years, and the vast majority of children with hearing loss are now served in their home school districts by a teacher who comes to the school for a designated period of time on a weekly basis (Johnson, 2002). Teachers who provide itinerant service often are giving students specific content-course academic support. They assist in preparation for exams, preteach complicated materials, and provide a great deal of consultative services to all of the general education teachers who work with their students. It is the itinerant teacher's responsibility to make sure the child is maintaining his academic standing in the general education environment. The itinerant teacher provides services to general education teachers to facilitate the student's growth within the inclusionary setting. There is much travel-time involved, and flexibility is a key attribute needed to be successful as an itinerant teacher of D/HH students (Klein & Glor-Scheib, 2001).

## Communication Philosophies

We have discussed the wide array of service delivery models; that is, the educational options available for students who are deaf or hard of hearing across the United States. Within these different models, there also exists a variety of communication philosophies. We will not support any one philosophy over another, but rather will briefly introduce those most commonly seen in deaf education today. Once the fundamental principles are outlined, the readers may assess how spoken communication fits within the framework of the communication philosophy in which they teach.

*Bilingual/Bicultural Approach.* The basic tenet of the **Bilingual/Bicultural approach** for teaching learners who are deaf is that American Sign Language (ASL) is the dominant language employed for academic and English language instruction. ASL is used for teaching content areas and English is taught as a second language. The bilingual model also stresses that the two languages (American Sign Language and spoken English) be kept separate in order to provide a more realistic communication environment. Speech is usually taught by a speech teacher and focuses primarily on spoken English rather than a simultaneous communication system. It is hoped that students in the Bilingual/Bicultural approach will develop ASL as their primary mode of communication and English (in the written form, spoken, or both) as a second language in communicating with the world around them (Nover & Andrews, 1998).

*Total Communication.* The **Total Communication** philosophy supports the use of appropriate combinations of auditory, oral, and manual methods of communication. The teacher often uses his voice as he signs what he is saying in English word order. This philosophy emphasizes learning English, both written and spoken, while also using a form of Manually Coded English, such as Signed English, Pidgin Signed English, or Conceptually Accurate Signed English to support speech. Usually, speech is taught by either the classroom teacher, a speech teacher, or by both. It is hoped that students in Total Communication programs will develop both sign and speech in communicating with the world around them.

*Auditory/Oral (A/O) Philosophy.* According to the **Auditory/Oral** philosophy, spoken English along with natural gestures are used in the classroom setting. The use of sign language is discouraged, but not reprimanded, in most of today's A/O classrooms. Here, students are encouraged to use their residual hearing, speechreading, and expressive speech. Most students receive individual tutoring in speech by the classroom teacher or a speech specialist. It is hoped that students in Auditory/Oral classrooms develop spoken English as their primary mode of communication with the world around them.

*Does Speech Fit?* Is there a place for teaching speech to deaf children who are in these various classroom settings and communicating via different philosophies? Yes, there is a place in *every* classroom for spoken communication, but the degree of emphasis will vary depending on the setting. The important point is that all forms of communication are valued, accepted, and reinforced in all settings.

## Working Evaluation

In order to be an effective teacher, you must have the kind of information that will allow you to make informed decisions regarding the student's needs. A spoken communication assessment is necessary to determine at what level to begin teaching. To that end, we have designed a new assessment instrument that works as both an assessment tool and a teaching plan.

# What Is in Part II?

In the following chapters, we will discuss how to:

- establish an open and supportive classroom environment
- evaluate the student's spoken communication skills
- set up a program based on the speech evaluation tool
- outline specific strategies that can be incorporated into the classroom or tutorial environment
- utilize instructional technology wherever possible in the various environments, and
- incorporate parents as full-fledged partners in the various classroom settings

We encourage all potential "speech teachers" to think creatively and keep an open mind as we examine the multitude of possibilities available in the many teachable moments during the school day.

*Chapter 5*

---

# Creating a Speech-Friendly Classroom

Few professionals would argue that when educating students who are deaf or hard of hearing, the single most important aspect to consider is communication. Without a solid language base, children have no way of relating to the world around them. It is imperative that every student has a strong understanding and ability to communicate easily with her family, friends, and peers. The classroom environment must be a place where students feel welcome, safe, and free to communicate with fellow students and teachers in a comfortable and natural manner. When a student walks into her classroom, the atmosphere must be accepting; the environment should be rich; and the mood, inviting. Students of all ages and hearing abilities want to feel like valuable members of their class, *their society*, at all times. People want to have the power and independence to control their environment and not be controlled within its walls.

## Beyond the Pullout Model

Traditionally, speech services for D/HH children have been delivered by a specialist who took the child out of the classroom for tutoring. Because the specialist generally pulled the student out of class and went to another location within the school, this service delivery model is called the pullout model. There are both advantages and disadvantages to this model. It is also important to weigh the cost-benefit ratio in deciding if this model is truly best for the child.

The major advantage of the traditional pullout model is that the child receives one-on-one tutoring with a trained professional. This one-on-one model provides the child with more individualized practice with speech. We believe that the disadvantages outweigh the advantages, however, and recommend bringing the program to the child, rather than taking her out of class. The disadvantages of the pullout model are:

- **Self-esteem.** The child who is constantly feeling singled out often senses that she is "different" when she just wants to fit in to the group.

- **Missed class work.** When the student is pulled out of class, she is missing valuable class time that will need to be made up later. Some teachers think they are helping the situation by having the student go to speech during "unimportant" times of the day, such as art, physical education, or recess. Just ask the child how unimportant these subjects are!
- **Speech unrelated to class work.** Unless the speech teacher and classroom teacher are working together, many speech practice sessions have little to do with the subjects that the child is learning about in school.
- **Communication abilities of the speech specialist.** Most SLPs have a great deal of knowledge about speech, but have only minimal training with deafness or sign language. Some well-meaning speech and language pathologists cannot communicate appropriately with their students.

We recommend that we blend what is good about the pullout program with what is good about the notion of "pushing-in." Let the SLP and the classroom teacher work together without pulling students individually out of class.

In this chapter, we will outline ways to make your classroom a friendly and welcoming one, full of communication in all of its forms. We will describe three different opportunities for spoken communication to be learned, practiced, and used pragmatically. Individual student goals may be learned during **tutoring time**, previously learned goals may be practiced and mastered during **group lessons**, and ongoing goals may be used during **transition times** and nonstructured daily activities.

| New skills | Practicing skills | Mastered & Ongoing Skills |
|---|---|---|
| Tutoring | Group lessons | Transition times |

# Tutoring Time: Classroom Centers

Many teachers have used the concept of centers in their classrooms. Centers are stations, or areas in the classroom where a certain skill is practiced. In a self-contained classroom, there may be as many centers as there are students. In a larger classroom, students may go to centers in pairs or small groups. Centers should be designed with activities that can be done independently, without the leadership of an adult. You may decide on centers that meet the needs of your teaching schedule and activities that enhance the subjects you teach. For instance, in a preschool classroom, there may be an activity about colors or shapes at the art center. In a third grade classroom, there may be an activity to practice keyboarding at the computer center. In sixth grade, there may be a journalism assignment to work on at the writing center. All centers can and should contain an element of communication. Table 5.1 (page 55) provides examples of activities at various classroom centers.

## Finding Time for Centers

Teachers constantly feel the crunch for time as they try to get through their daily schedule. Continual interruptions, holidays, assemblies, library time, and so on, all tend to frustrate the teacher in her effort to accomplish a great deal in a short day. Although these distractions from the schedule are deemed important, they do wreak havoc on a teacher's plan. The use of centers is helpful in this regard, as students can make up missed work later in a day during center time. We find that "center-time" often is the students' favorite period of the day.

Teachers know that their days are filled with teaching the required content areas, and some believe that there is no time left to fit in centers. Teachers generally divide a typical thirty-minute lesson into demonstration, group activity, and individual practice. By using center-focused instruction, you teach the demonstration and group activity, and save the ten minutes of individual practice for center time, as shown in the revised daily schedule in Figure 5.1 (see page 56).

## The Communications Center

Every classroom should have a communications center. There are a number of creative ways to make your communications center a popular place to work and learn. Keep your sign language dictionary, flash cards, TTY, Language

| *Table 5.1.* **Examples of instructional centers.** | |
| --- | --- |
| **Computers** | **Writing** |
| Games | Spelling |
| Journals | English |
| Assignments | Grammar |
| Keyboarding | Journalism |
| Word processing | Dictionary skills |
| **Reading** | **Science** |
| Free reading | Experiments |
| Guided reading | Microscopes |
| Storytelling | Sorting |
| Reader's theater | Observations |
| **Math** | **Art** |
| Games | Drawing |
| Worksheets | Painting |
| Homework helpers | Crafts |
| **Communications** | |
| Phonetic/phonologic speech practice | |
| Role-playing | |
| TTY practice | |

Master, tape recorders, and communication games and activities handy at this center. This is where the teacher or SLP can set up a tutoring area for spoken communication. If there are hearing students in the class, they may learn new sign language or vocabulary words, or learn various pragmatic skills such as making social introductions. Activities for use in the communication center are endless.

The communications center is where the speech teacher can choose to work individually with each student. Depending on the age of the students, the activities in this center will vary. Students who are between the ages of three and seven crave the individual attention and enjoy working one-on-one with their teacher. Students who are between eight and thirteen years of age are less likely to desire individual attention, so rather than force them to "come to speech," use a different approach.

Students may want to use the communications center to work in pairs playing barrier games or other communication-based activities. Activities such as "TV Critic/Reviewer," which encourages discussing last night's favorite sit-com, elicits pragmatic language that is important and relevant to students' lives.

The teacher or speech and language pathologist acts as facilitator and casual observer, creating new opportunities for communication between students and those around them. It is vitally important that this center be a positive place, where the students feel comfortable and accepted. There must be a strong element of trust between student and teacher in order for learning to take place. Students should never feel corrected or "put down" for any attempts made in communication. Taking a positive approach with your students toward their communication efforts will always result in cooperative and collaborative work at the communications center.

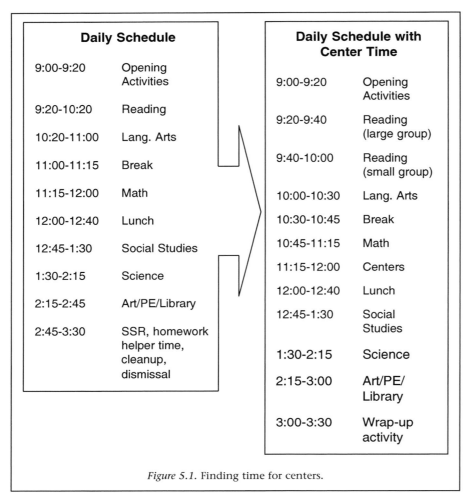

**Daily Schedule**

| 9:00-9:20 | Opening Activities |
| 9:20-10:20 | Reading |
| 10:20-11:00 | Lang. Arts |
| 11:00-11:15 | Break |
| 11:15-12:00 | Math |
| 12:00-12:40 | Lunch |
| 12:45-1:30 | Social Studies |
| 1:30-2:15 | Science |
| 2:15-2:45 | Art/PE/Library |
| 2:45-3:30 | SSR, homework helper time, cleanup, dismissal |

**Daily Schedule with Center Time**

| 9:00-9:20 | Opening Activities |
| 9:20-9:40 | Reading (large group) |
| 9:40-10:00 | Reading (small group) |
| 10:00-10:30 | Lang. Arts |
| 10:30-10:45 | Break |
| 10:45-11:15 | Math |
| 11:15-12:00 | Centers |
| 12:00-12:40 | Lunch |
| 12:45-1:30 | Social Studies |
| 1:30-2:15 | Science |
| 2:15-3:00 | Art/PE/Library |
| 3:00-3:30 | Wrap-up activity |

*Figure 5.1.* Finding time for centers.

## Speech in High School

High school age deaf and hard of hearing students are often tired of working on their spoken communication skills, particularly if most of their work was the pullout drill-and-practice type of speech instruction. As members of the team, it is important that teachers respect the opinions of these students. It is not our goal to have students feel they have a life sentence with a speech tutor! Rather, we should help this age student understand that the assistance is there for them if they want it.

Many high school students choose to return to work with a speech teacher when they become more secure with themselves and their communication style, or if they discover that they have a real need to improve their skills. With maturation they often realize that the speech teacher can help them develop more sophisticated communication skills. Job interviews, driver's license exams, prom date protocol, and college exams and applications are all topics that serve as motivators to work on spoken communication skills. It is important for the high school-level teacher to be aware of the informal language and up-to-date vocabulary that is common among teenagers and be prepared to enhance its use. Understanding and using the current vernacular demonstrates respect for the students as well as a willingness to communicate in "their" language.

The benefits of having one-on-one time with students are, at times, invaluable. Students who recall a positive relationship with teachers as human beings with whom they can relate will grow up with good feelings about their education. Students who recall a comfortable process of communication with their teacher, a safe time when their communication was given merit and importance, that what they had to say was more remarkable than how they said it, will be more well adjusted and comfortable dealing with challenging communicative environments.

# Daily Lesson Time

Just as individual goals can be learned during center-time, previously learned goals can be practiced during daily lessons. As teachers, we are sometimes expected to be everything to everyone. It is not the intention here to suggest that you must meet these impossible demands. A skilled teacher, however, will be adept at incorporating many objectives into one lesson. There will often be carryover in a history lesson that ties into what students are learning in reading, spelling, English, and other content areas. Although this is not considered a simple task, experienced teachers know that teaching across the curriculum is necessary and worthwhile in order for students to learn at a deeper level.

In terms of speech production, daily lessons are not the time to teach new or unfamiliar speech sounds but to practice previously learned sounds and skills. In this context, it is not difficult to tie spoken communication objectives into daily lesson plans. Let us talk about three different examples that might be done in a classroom for young children (grades preschool-2), intermediate students (grades 3-6), and secondary students (grades 7-12).

---

**Not-So-Hypothetical: Grades P-2**

In a math lesson for first graders, the objective for the day is that students will begin to add one-digit numbers. Mr. Diaz is explaining the concept on the board and students are coming up to the board to solve problems. When they have each completed their problem, he asks the students to read the number sentences that they have written to the class. One student begins, "Four plus five equals nine." He had solved the problem correctly and the teacher felt confident that he understood the concept of simple addition. Mr. Diaz points out to the students the number sentence that was just read and asks if they can tell the beginning sound of the words *four* and *five.* He then asks the children if they know how to spell the word *four.* He continues asking questions: "What sounds do you recognize? Who can fingerspell the word? Who can show me the sign for the word? Who can show me what it looks like on your mouth? Who can say, 'fffff'? Does it have any voice? Can you feel the air coming out when you put your finger up in front of your lips?"

---

Mr. Diaz just incorporated a simple speech practice activity into a math lesson. Did he lose time? Perhaps one minute of time was spent grasping this teachable moment; the rewards, on the other hand, were great. The students were not corrected, did not feel isolated or picked on, and had an opportunity to practice a valuable lesson. Practicing previously learned knowledge only helps to solidify the information in the students' minds.

---

**Not-So-Hypothetical: Intermediate**

In a fifth grade classroom, students are studying new vocabulary for a social studies unit. Mrs. Goldstein has written ten new words on the board, and the students are looking up the words in the dictionary and reporting back their findings. She makes a chart with the new words going down the left side of the paper. She adds columns for (1) the part of speech, (2) the definition, and (3) the pronunciation. As the students discuss the results of their findings, they will have new information about the words that they learned. Mrs. Goldstein describes how to use the pronunciation key in the dictionary as the students fill out the column on pronunciation. On the

*cont.*

---

board, she takes one of the words and breaks it into syllables, talking about the English spelling, what it looks like in speech-reading, and the stress that each syllable takes. Mrs. Goldstein says, "Let's look at the word *revolution*. What does the word mean? How do you sign the word? How do you spell this word? What is the part of speech? Break up the word into syllables. According to the dictionary, which syllables get the stress?" (/rev'a loo'-sh∂n/) Mrs. Goldstein shows the students that there are four syllables and the first and third get the stress. She discusses how, in English, the suffix *-tion* is pronounced "sh∂n" with no stress.

Even if a student doesn't use her voice in communication, Mrs. Goldstein taught a valuable lesson about spoken English.

**Not-So-Hypothetical: High School**
In high school biology, Mr. O'Brien's class is learning about parts of the cell. One of the vocabulary words is *golgi,* and neither the teacher nor any of the students know how it is pronounced. Mr. O'Brien asks one of the students to go to the dictionary and look up the word and tell him how it is pronounced. The students learn a) that not all hearing adults know how all English words are pronounced, and b) how answers can be found by using references.

Teaching across the curriculum is a strategy used by most skilled teachers in any classroom. By incorporating spoken English as another element of the curriculum, the students have more opportunities to practice the skills they are learning.

# Transition Times

There are many opportunities during the day for spoken communication to be used. The times between classes, before and after recess, lining up, playtime, small group activities, class parties, or discussions, are all considered transition times or unstructured times of the day. It is totally unacceptable to correct speech during these times of the day. If a student elects to use speech during these times, it is because she feels secure and safe in her environment. Can you imagine running in from the playground, with an exciting story, only to be interrupted repeatedly by your teacher, constantly correcting your speech?!

Many teachable moments come up naturally, some of which can be preplanned into your classroom, during times of transition. By encouraging spoken communication in a variety of situations, students have the chance to use the skills they have learned during individual tutoring time and practiced during daily lessons.

**Not-So-Hypothetical**
While lining up for lunch, the kindergarten teacher reviews the lunch menu for the day. "What are you going to have for lunch today?" the teacher asks. "I want the hamburger!" answers one student. The teacher says, "Raise your hand if you're going to have the hamburger." She has the class practice saying "ham' bur ger" together as a group. She shows the class a picture, then has them review the sign, and say the word again. Then they begin walking together to lunch.

**Not-So-Hypothetical**

A third grade teacher gives her class new vocabulary words from the reading story. Different students are working on different sounds in speech and are not expected to be able to say the same words as other students in the class. From a list of unfamiliar words, they may choose ten new words that they would like to learn to say and use in a sentence. The teacher introduces a buddy system whereby if Student A uses a new word in a sentence correctly, she will get an extra credit point. If her buddy, Student B, listens to her use it correctly, she will act as a witness and receive a point as well. This is an ongoing activity than can take place during any transition period, e.g., recess, riding the bus, free time, and so forth.

Creating a speech-friendly classroom is the first key in establishing the amiable atmosphere that every teacher and student want to have. Think about your students not as children who will remain this age forever, but as the young adults, teachers, and professionals that they will become. It is clear that a non-threatening, communication-friendly classroom environment will add to a student's ability to become a well-adjusted communicator in all environments. Having pleasurable memories of school is an added bonus.

# Summary

In this chapter we discussed the importance of creating an environment that is inviting and conducive to communication. Of tantamount importance is that the student feels comfortable, unthreatened, and willing to take a chance communicating regardless of her level of speech intelligibility.

We also addressed the multiple opportunities available throughout the day to involve students directly in speech activities. The activities can occur at any of three levels of speech production. The use of instructional centers in the classroom allows for the teacher, SLP, or the student alone to work on her phonetic and phonologic-level skills. Several Not-So-Hypothetical scenarios were presented to illustrate quick strategies that encourage phonologic-level practice during instructional activities. And finally, opportunities for pragmatic-level practice were highlighted during daily transition activities.

In each of these cases, the spoken communication practice was easily woven into the fabric of the daily classroom routines. Teachers seized teachable moments and students had a natural and spontaneous opportunity to enhance their spoken communication skills.

Regardless of the particular service delivery model of instruction, whether you are in an inclusive setting or a self-contained school for D/HH children, these strategies for creating a speech-friendly classroom setting will work for you and your students.

# Chapter 5 Topics for Discussion

1.  Design a communications center activity that enables second grade students to focus on producing polysyllabic words starting with the *f* sound.

2.  Create a scenario in which a child has the opportunity to practice asking questions during a social studies lesson.

3.  You encounter a classroom that encourages negative competition in the form of ability groupings. The students who are the least verbal are in the lowest group and everybody in the class knows it. The children in this group don't openly communicate very often in class or out of class. How might you collaborate with this classroom teacher to establish a more speech-friendly classroom for your student, who is in the lowest ability group?

# *Chapter 6*

# Evaluation

Any speech program should begin with a basic evaluation to learn each student's functional use of spoken communication. Customarily, when teachers are faced with the task of evaluation, they become bogged down in the process because it is so time-consuming. Many teachers believe their skills are inadequate; others believe the responsibility of evaluation belongs with another professional (Otis-Wilborn, 1992). The evaluation phase need not be considered an insurmountable chore. The main purpose in giving a speech evaluation is to determine where to begin your speech program.

In this chapter, we will offer a new approach to evaluating the spoken communication skills of students who are deaf or hard of hearing. We will outline and describe two types of evaluations: the Oral Peripheral Examination and the Student Speech Record.* The Oral Peripheral Exam is given to young students who have never participated in speech before. The Student Speech Record is an ongoing evaluation given once at the beginning of the school year and then updated in January and May. In addition, we refer you to Appendix C: Vendors of Instructional Materials and Assistive Devices, which provides a reference of evaluation tools and materials that are frequently used in assessing the spoken communication abilities of D/HH children.

---

* The Oral Peripheral Examination Form and the Student Speech Record are available separately from Butte Publications.

# Finding Time for the Evaluation

In the previous chapter, it was suggested that each classroom schedule allow time to have centers. It is during this time that you may complete your speech evaluations. You will find that you will need approximately five minutes per child to give the Oral Peripheral Exam and approximately ten minutes for the Student Speech Record. Therefore, if your centers are designed for ten-minute activities, you may wish to use two days to complete the evaluations. It is wise to begin as soon as possible after school starts in the fall, so that you can get right to the business of teaching, without using up excessive time on testing. Remember that the purpose of evaluation is to establish teaching goals. This may be done quickly, yet thoroughly, in a reasonable amount of time.

# Oral Peripheral Examination

The purpose of the Oral Peripheral Examination is to determine if there are any physical abnormalities in the areas in and around the mouth, which may preclude normal speech production. This exam provides the speech teachers with information regarding the student's motoric ability to produce speech. Difficulties in motor or phonetic-level production will have a significant impact on spoken communication skills in general. If the examiner detects an abnormality that is correctable, he should notify the parents, who will decide on the action to be taken.

Figure 6.1 is a blank copy of the Oral Peripheral Examination checklist. The Oral Peripheral Examination is relatively simple and may be carried out by any adult on the team with the instructions presented here. As noted above, this is a good use for a center-time activity.

**Oral Peripheral Examination Form**

Name _____    Date _____    Age _____

School _____    Evaluator _____    Teacher _____

| Structure | No Concern | Area of Concern | Notations | | No Concern | Area of Concern | Notations |
|---|---|---|---|---|---|---|---|
| **FACE** | | | | **TEETH** | | | |
| Facial symmetry | | | | Braces | | | |
| Any paralysis | | | | Missing teeth | | | |
| Physical abnormalities | | | | Malocclusion (overbite) | | | |
| Mouth breather | | | | Mesioclusion (underbite) | | | |
| **LIPS** | | | | Spaces - teeth | | | |
| Spread lips-smile | | | | **TONGUE** | | | |
| Round lips-pucker | | | | Points tongue | | | |
| Touch upper and lower lips | | | | Touches palate | | | |
| **NOSE** | | | | Retracts tongue | | | |
| Congested | | | | Tongue lays flat | | | |
| Crooked septum | | | | Tip behind upper front teeth | | | |
| Hypernasal resonance | | | | Short frenum | | | |
| Denasal resonance | | | | Licks lips in circle | | | |
| **PALATE AND VELUM** | | | | Touches side to side outside mouth | | | |
| High-narrow palate | | | | Licks a lollipop | | | |
| Cleft | | | | Tongue thrust during swallowing | | | |
| Bifid uvula | | | | **FUNCTIONS** | | | |
| Velopharyngeal port movement | | | | Blows out candle | | | |
| **LARYNX** | | | | Blows up balloon | | | |
| Aphonic (no voice) | | | | Drinks through a straw | | | |
| Breathy voice | | | | | | | |
| Husky/raspy voice | | | | | | | |

*Figure 6.1.* Oral Peripheral Examination Form.

## Administering the Oral Peripheral Examination

The Oral Peripheral Exam is given to young children (under six years old) or to older children beginning a new program. The exam does not need to be given more than once unless a significant change occurs in the student's physical condition that relates to speech production.

During the Oral Peripheral Examination, the evaluator observes the student's face, lips, nose, hard palate, soft palate, teeth, and tongue, and listens to his voice quality as noted on the checklist. A few materials are needed to complete the Oral Peripheral Examination, including a balloon, a lighter and candle, a lollipop, a straw, and a cup of water.

As you begin, explain to the child that he will be imitating what you are doing. If you spread your lips into a smile, the child should imitate this behavior. If you touch your lips repeatedly with the tip of your tongue, he should do the same. It is not uncommon for young children to have missing teeth, and that should be noted where appropriate on the Oral Peripheral Evaluation form. In general, missing teeth will not significantly impact a student's ability to produce speech sounds. The evaluator completes the checklist by marking the columns "No Concern" or "Area of Concern" as the child finishes each task.

# The Student Speech Record (SSR)

The Student Speech Record is designed to be an evaluation tool as well as a teaching plan. This form should be completed once at the beginning of the school year after completing the Oral Peripheral Exam, and it should be updated twice during the year. This record provides a quick, simple way to determine teaching objectives. For your reference, see Figure 6.2 (pages 1–3) for a blank form of the SSR.

---

**STUDENT SPEECH RECORD***

_____     _____     _____
Student          School Year          Evaluator

_____     _____
Student's Age      Student's Grade

Multidisciplinary Team Members:

(Name)               (Title)

_____ , _____

_____ , _____          *For a more detailed description
                                              and directions for how to
_____ , _____          administer this evaluation,
                                              refer to *Spoken Communication
_____ , _____          for Students Who Are Deaf or Hard of
                                              Hearing: A Multidisciplinary Approach*
_____ , _____

*Figure 6.2.* Student Speech Record (page 1).

**Nonverbal Communication**

*Observe each of the skills listed and determine how comfortable the student is with each skill. Plot the skills in the columns on the right. Check off the boxes on the left.*

**Suprasegmental Aspects**

*Observe the student's ability to vocalize, to vary the length of sound, to raise and lower his intensity, and to vary his intonation. Plot skills in columns on right. Check off boxes on left.*

**Vowel and Diphthongs**

*Begin testing each vowel sound by coarticulating it with a known consonant. Model in sustained and repeated syllables to obtain a complete sample of the student's abilities.*

**Consonants**

*Begin testing each consonant sound by coarticulating it with a known vowel. Model in sustained and repeated syllables to obtain a complete sample of the student's abilities.*

| PHONETIC | PHONOLOGIC | PRAGMATIC |
|---|---|---|
| *This is considered the teaching/learning level.* | *This is considered the practice level.* | *This is considered the comfort level.* |
| *If a sound needs to be taught and learned, it is placed in this column.* | *A sound that has been introduced and learned, but is not fully mastered, is placed in this column.* | *If a skill or sound has been learned and practiced, and the student feels comfortable using this in his everyday spoken communication, the skill is placed in this column.* |
| *Teacher generally works on a one-to-one level with the student.* | *Teacher can tutor or incorporate into daily lessons.* | |
| *There should be approximately five sounds at one time at this level.* | *Parents can support at home.* | *Parents, teachers, and the student himself can monitor, support, and encourage use of this skill.* |
| | *Communication Books may be used.* | |

**SAMPLE**

| PHONETIC | PHONOLOGIC | PRAGMATIC |
|---|---|---|
| i | turn-taking | eye contact |
| m | intonation | b |
| f | p | a |
| t | u | |
| o | | |

*Figure 6.2.* Student Speech Record (page 2).

---

**STUDENT SPEECH RECORD**

Name _____
Evaluator _____
Date _____

**Nonverbal Communication**

attention ☐
turn-taking ☐
eye contact ☐
breath support ☐

**Suprasegmental Aspects**

vocalization ☐
duration ☐
intensity ☐
intonation ☐

**Vowel and Diphthongs**

a ☐  u ☐  aʊ☐  o ☐  ʌ ☐
ɪ ☐  ɛ ☐  i ☐  ɔɪ☐  æ ☐  ʊ ☐
eɪ ☐  aɪ ☐  ɝ ☐

**Consonants**

p ☐  f ☐  θ ☐  t ☐  h ☐
b ☐  v ☐  ð ☐  d ☐  w ☐
m ☐  n ☐  ŋ ☐  j ☐
ʃ ☐  s ☐  ʧ ☐  k ☐  l ☐
ʒ ☐  z ☐  ʤ ☐  g ☐  r ☐

| PHONETIC | PHONOLOGIC | PRAGMATIC |
|---|---|---|
| | | |

*Figure 6.2.* Student Speech Record (page 3).

## Components of the Student Speech Record

The SSR was developed to assess all of the components that make up spoken language production. There are four components of the Student Speech Record: nonverbal communication, suprasegmentals, vowels and diphthongs, and consonants. There are also three levels of speech production into which these components should be sorted: phonetic, phonologic, and pragmatic.

***Nonverbal Communication.*** Effective communicators demonstrate good nonverbal skills. Observe the student's nonverbal communication skills. Does the student have an adequate attention span? Does he understand the concept of taking turns? Can the student maintain eye contact? Does he have adequate breath support? If you answer "no" to any of these questions, it is important to note this on the SSR. These are prerequisite skills for the development of good spoken communication. A child must develop these skills first, if spoken language is to develop.

***Suprasegmental Aspects.*** As you recall, the suprasegmental or prosodic aspects of speech include intonation, pitch, and intensity. Will the child vocalize on demand? Can the student vary the duration, intensity, and intonation of his voice? If the student has difficulty with any of these skills, each of which is also a fundamental of good spoken language production, mark it on the SSR.

***Vowels and Diphthongs.*** An evaluation of a student's ability to produce vowels and diphthongs is a good indicator of the ability to manipulate the primary organ of articulation, the tongue. Difficulty in producing vowel sounds in English will have a direct effect on the overall intelligibility of a person's speech skills. When evaluating vowels and consonants, it is wise to use the International Phonetic Alphabet (IPA) symbols. These clearly indicate exactly what the student is producing when he uses speech. Refer to the International Phonetic Alphabet chart (Figure 6.3) if you are unfamiliar with these symbols.

| English | IPA | Key Words |
|---|---|---|
| h | /h/ | house |
| wh | /hw/ | when |
| p | /p/ | pie/top |
| t | /t/ | tie/hat |
| k | /k/ | kite/sock |
| f | /f/ | fine/if |
| th[1] | /θ/ | thin, mouth |
| s | /s/ | sun, grass |
| sh | /ʃ/ | ship, dish |
| ch | /ʧ/ | chime, match |
| w- | /w/ | win |
| b | /b/ | boy, cab |
| d | /d/ | dog, mad |
| g | /g/ | game/hug |
| v | /v/ | voice, cave |
| th[2] | /ð/ | them, bathe |
| z | /z/ | zoo, buzz |
| zh | /ʒ/ | genre, garage |
| j | /ʤ/ | john, fudge |
| m | /m/ | mop, hum |
| n | /n/ | nose, line |
| ng | /ŋ/ | hanger, hung |
| l | /l/ | laugh, ball |
| r | /r/ | race |
| y- | /j/ | yellow |
| oo | /u/ | boot |
| -oo- | /ʊ/ | hook |
| aw | /ɔ/ | awful |
| ee | /i/ | eat |
| -i- | /ɪ/ | if |
| -e- | /ɛ/ | end |
| -a- | /æ/ | at |
| -o- | /ɑ/ | odd |
| -u- | /ʌ/ | up |
| -u- | /ə/ | above |
| ur | /ɝ/ | earth |
| a-e | /eɪ/ | made |
| i-e | /aɪ/ | high |
| oa | /o/ | boat |
| oi | /ɔɪ/ | coin |
| u-e | /ju/ | use |
| ou | /aʊ/ | out |
| er | /ɚ/ | mother |

*Figure 6.3.* International Phonetic Alphabet (IPA) Chart.

***Consonants.*** The consonants are the final component of the SSR. Evaluation of the consonants allows the speech teacher to determine the nature of difficulty the student may have in terms of his speech production. Can the student build up the right amount of oral pressure to produce a plosive speech sound? Does the student have control of the velum for the production of nasal sounds? As each group of consonant sounds is evaluated, these questions should be kept in mind and noted as necessary on the SSR.

## Levels of Speech Production

We can divide spoken communication into three different levels of speech production: the **Phonetic**, the **Phonologic**, and the **Pragmatic**. As you look at the Student Speech Record, notice the columns marked Phonetic, Phonologic, and Pragmatic on pages 2 and 3. These three levels of speech production are a somewhat subjective demarcation of the student's level of progress along a continuum, as suggested below:

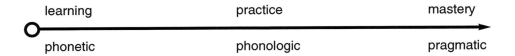

| learning | practice | mastery |
|---|---|---|
| phonetic | phonologic | pragmatic |

When a person learns any new skill, there is a natural progression from learning, to practice, and finally, mastery. Just as you wouldn't send a beginning skier down the expert slope, neither would you expect a student who is deaf to instantly begin using recently learned speech sounds in complete sentences. The practice stage is imperative in any newly acquired skill. When learning spoken communication skills, a student must go through the same process. A detailed description of the three levels of speech production follows.

***Phonetic.*** At the phonetic level of speech, sounds are produced as specific and sometimes isolated phonemes. Here, sounds have no linguistic meaning and are considered nonsense syllables. Speech sound production at the phonetic level is strictly a motor production task. The student learns the articulation, placement, and voice qualities of various sounds before they are put into meaningful words. In general, if a child has appropriate amplification and has been exposed to quality acoustic input, the need for specific phonetic-level training is significantly reduced (Ling, 1989).

In some cases, the teacher of the deaf or the speech and language pathologist will need to teach sounds at the phonetic level. This level is best taught during individual tutoring time. When making the initial speech evaluation, the sounds that need to be specifically *taught* as motor tasks are placed in the Phonetic column.

***Phonologic.*** The phonologic level refers to sounds that have been taught or previously produced at the phonetic level, but now require contextual practice. The sound is integrated into meaningful language already in the child's repertoire. Sounds taught in the phonetic level as nonsense syllables are put into words, phrases, and sentences that have meaning for the child. The purpose of phonologic-level practice is to help the child reach a level of automaticity (Ling, 1976) in speech production. We want the child to be able to speak automatically without having to think about how or what he wants to say.

When working at the phonologic level, the sound /m/ that was taught in the phonetic level now becomes "mom" and is paired with the sign for MOTHER, the finger-spelling m-o-m, and if age-appropriate, the written word. Teachers, parents, teacher aides, and siblings should all participate in phonologic-level practice. When completing the initial Student Speech Record evaluation, the sounds that need to be *practiced* are placed in the Phonologic column.

***Pragmatic.*** The pragmatic level in the evaluation is for sounds that have been taught and practiced and are now considered automatic for the child. At this level, the child rarely needs to think about how a sound is produced; it just naturally occurs in his spontaneous speech. The child usually monitors his own speech and does not need reminding from others. The pragmatic level may be considered the comfort zone, where the student does not consciously work at speech. When making the initial speech evaluation, the sounds that are easily *produced* in general conversation are placed in the Pragmatic column.

## Determining the Level for Teaching

Throughout the Student Speech Record evaluation, you will be plotting various sounds or skills into the appropriate columns. When you have five sounds or skills listed in the Phonetic column, the Student Speech Record is complete. A beginner may not have anything listed in the Pragmatic column. Other students, who are more comfortable with spoken communication, may have many skills listed. Regardless of the student's level, when five sounds or skills are placed in the Phonetic column, you have a place to begin teaching.

---

**Not-So-Hypothetical**

As I went to meet six-year-old Shari for the first time, she eagerly came with me for the "game" that we were going to play. The first thing I noticed about her communication was that she had a very short attention span. She saw things and pointed to them, but didn't sign the names of things or wait to see if I would tell her the names for them. When we sat down and I began to explain what we were going to do, I noticed that she was still looking all over the room and did not look at me for any great length of time. I noted on the SSR that we would put "maintains attention" and "maintains eye contact" as the first goals in the Phonetic column. When we played with our voices, I added "vocalization" and "duration" as well. As she learned to experiment more with her voice, I added the vowels /a/ and /u/ and the consonants /p/ and /f/. The evaluation was completed in a few short minutes and I now had six goals on which I could plan my speech lessons for Shari.

When I met six-year-old Andre for the first time, I noted that he was quite the chatterbox. He pointed to things and signed their names; he put together three- or four-word phrases and asked me questions and then waited for my responses. We "established rapport" while walking to the room for the evaluation. By the time we sat down to play the "game," I had already assessed that he would not need any goals for nonverbal communication and I placed these in the Pragmatic column. As I explained what we were going to do, I determined that he knew how to vocalize and how to vary the intensity and duration of his voice. Those items were also placed in the Pragmatic column. He quickly understood how to play the game and modeled all of my examples. After only five minutes, we had two vowels and four consonant sounds written in the Phonetic column, several vowels and consonants in the Phonologic column, and the nonverbal and suprasegmental items in the Pragmatic column. The evaluation was complete and we were ready to begin Andre's speech program.

***Get a Good Sample.*** When evaluating any of the sounds, you must get a good sample in order to assess the student's comfort level. If you model "baaa" and the student repeats "baaa" with reasonable clarity, would you automatically place the /b/ sound in the pragmatic column? You would be making a hasty decision using only one small clue if you did. Upon further investigation, you may find that he can say the /b/ at the beginning of a syllable, but only with the vowel /a/. It is important to get as much information as possible by getting a lengthier sample. Therefore, give the sound using multiple vowels and in varying positions in the syllable:   ba – bababa – be – bebebe – ebebeb – ubu – ububububu – and so on. Now, instead of having one small piece of information, you have a more complete idea of how easily the student can produce the sound /b/.

***Procedures for Giving the SSR.*** The multidisciplinary team should make the determination of who is best qualified to administer the Student Speech Record. Once the team has determined who will be giving the evaluation, you [Note that we refer to the evaluator as *you* for ease of reading.—Authors] will follow these important steps:

- Establish rapport
- Explain modeling
- Evaluate nonverbal communication
- Evaluate vowel production
- Evaluate consonant production

Use a pencil as you complete page 3 of the Student Speech Record. You may check off each skill in the boxes on the left as you evaluate the student's production. After you evaluate each skill on the left, write these skills in the columns on the right when you decide how well the student can produce them. If the student struggles with a skill, place it in the Phonetic column; if he can produce it but needs practice, write it in the Phonologic column; and if the student passes this skill with ease, it will go into the Pragmatic column.

Begin by explaining the concept of modeling. You will point to yourself when it's your turn and you will point to the student when it's his turn. The only things that the student needs to do are to watch your model and to imitate what you say. You may also wish to touch the child's shoulder gently to indicate when it is his turn and encourage auditory concentration. Give an example to demonstrate what you mean.

The SSR evaluation begins at the level of nonverbal communication. If a student is unable to maintain eye contact, stay focused, or control the breath stream, these difficulties should be noted in the Phonetic column. If the child demonstrates these skills, but they are not consistent, place them into the Phonologic column. This means the skills still require practice. If you feel these skills are natural to the child and he uses them without thinking, you should place them in the Pragmatic column.

Move on to the suprasegmental aspects part of the evaluation. Ask the student to imitate syllables using different intensity, duration, and rhythm. If the student is unable to imitate these skills, mark them in the Phonetic column. These are skills that must be learned. Skills that are present but require practice should be noted in the Phonologic column. If the child can produce all of the suprasegmental skills with ease and comfort, you should list them in the Pragmatic column.

The vowels and diphthongs are evaluated next. Begin with the /a/ sound on the left side of the box and move to the right. These sounds are plotted from left to right and top to bottom with the easier sounds first, followed by those that are increasingly difficult for most deaf speakers. As you give the cue, remember to coarticulate with a developmentally easy consonant sound; for example, the sound /b/, or a sound that you have already heard the student use consistently. Coarticulation is combining a consonant with a vowel sound. Coarticulation allows you to produce the sound as it might appear normally in spoken English; sounds in isolation rarely appear in natural speech. As you listen to the child's production of the sound, you will *only* listen to the vowel sound. When the student repeats your model, even though the consonant may be incorrect, if the vowel sound is correct, the vowel is noted either under the Phonologic column if it still requires practice, or under the Pragmatic column if it is consistently correct. The evaluation of vowels and diphthongs should be finished when there are two or three plotted in the Phonetic column.

The final component of the SSR evaluation involves the consonants. The consonants are evaluated in much the same way as the vowels. Remember that in this category, you are *only* listening for the consonant being evaluated. Select a few vowels that the child can say easily, usually the /a/, /o/, or /u/ sounds. The consonant sound order has again been arranged by what seems to be the easier to the more difficult sounds. Move from left to right and top to bottom until you have three or four consonant sounds in the Phonetic column.

Continue evaluating the student until you have the desired number of teaching objectives. The Phonologic and Pragmatic columns will fill up quickly as more goals are mastered. More experienced speakers may start with a large number of sounds already in the Phonologic and Pragmatic columns. In that case, the work focuses on the skills that have yet to be developed.

***Points to Remember while Evaluating.*** The order of the sounds is less important than determining the sounds to teach. For example, if you are testing the voiceless /th/ sound and the child responds with an /s/ sound, you may decide to evaluate the /s/ sound instead. Seize the moment! Use the student's strengths; he may surprise you. Come back later to the voiceless /th/ sound and show the student visually if necessary.

When the evaluation is complete, your Student Speech Record serves as your goal sheet and you are ready to teach directly from this form. See Figure 6.4 (page 70) for a completed Student Speech Record. As objectives in the Phonetic column are taught and mastered, they will be moved to the Phonologic column by drawing an arrow through the sounds and rewriting them in the next column. Writing a date on the arrow helps to track the student's progress. When an objective is moved from the Phonetic to the Phonologic column, evaluate the next skill from the boxes on the left, always keeping five objectives in the Phonetic column at any time. This is a working record system and keeps the evaluation process an ongoing one. Refer to Figure 6.5 (page 70) to see what the Student Speech Record in Figure 6.4 might look like after one month.

***An Example SSR Dialogue.*** The following dialogue sequence demonstrates the administration of a Student Speech Record Evaluation.

- Select a quiet space with two chairs.
- Arrange the seats in the "love-seat" position: chairs face each other but are side-by-side, allowing for the optimal auditory and visual signals.
- Put the child at ease by casually talking to him and explaining what you will be doing.
- Refer to this activity as a game, never a test.
- Give the Ling Six Sound Test: ask the student to clap when he hears the sounds /m, a, u, i, ʃ, s/.
- Explain the concept of modeling: "We will take turns and you just copy whatever I say."

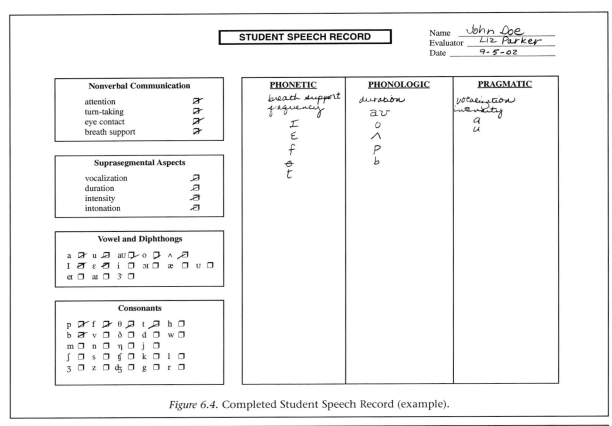

*Figure 6.4.* Completed Student Speech Record (example).

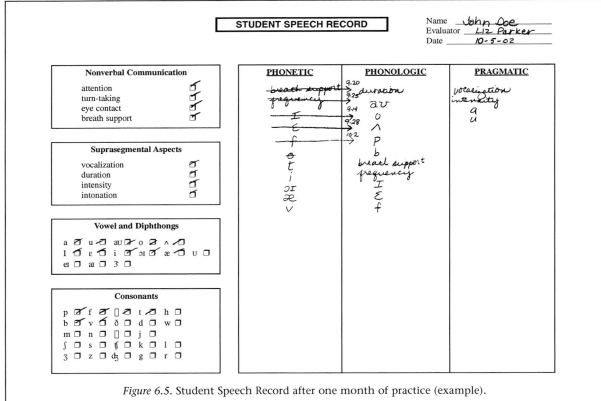

*Figure 6.5.* Student Speech Record after one month of practice (example).

- Begin with the **Nonverbal Communication** skills. Note whether or not the child can attend to you, can understand the basic turn-taking qualities of communication, can maintain eye contact, and has adequate breath support. If any of these skills needs to be taught or practiced, plot it in the appropriate column on the SSR.
- Evaluate the **Suprasegmental Aspects** of speech by seeing if the student can vocalize on demand, maintain duration of a sound, vary the intensity of his voice, and vary the intonation (pitch) of his voice. The following script suggests what the evaluation may sound like, but *any consonant-vowel combination may be used to assess this area.* Remember to listen *only* for the suprasegmental aspects at this time.

> Teacher model: /baaaaaaaaaaaaaa/ (duration, long)
> 　　　　　　(Student repeats.)
> Teacher model: /wu　wu　wu/ (duration, short)
> 　　　　　　(Student repeats.)
> Teacher model: /fi　fi　fiiiiiiiiii/ (duration, varied)
> 　　　　　　(Student repeats.)
> Teacher model: /ta ta ta/ (intensity, quiet)
> 　　　　　　(Student repeats.)
> Teacher model: /bu　bu　bu/ (intensity, loud)
> 　　　　　　(Student repeats.)
> Teacher model: /ma　ma　ma　ma/ (intensity, varied)
> 　　　　　　(Student repeats.)

- Assess the student's production of **Vowels** and **Diphthongs**. Select a simple consonant with which to coarticulate, for example, /p/:

> Teacher model : /paaaaaa/
> 　　　(Student repeats.)
> Teacher model: /papapapa/
> 　　　(Student repeats.)
> Teacher model: /puuuuuuu/
> 　　　(Student repeats.)
> Teacher model: /pupupupu/
> 　　　(Student repeats.)

Mark the vowel sounds in the correct column, remembering to listen *only* for the vowel production. If all the vowels are correct and do not need practice, list them in the Pragmatic column and move on. Continue modeling this way until two or three vowel sounds have been plotted in the Phonetic column. You do not need to assess all of the vowel sounds; stop when two or three goals have been identified.

- Assess the student's production of **Consonants**. Use a variety of simple vowels with which to coarticulate, for example, /o/ or /u/, and interchange them. Be sure to prolong the duration of fricative sounds to ensure the student's perception of the sound:

> Teacher model: /po/
> 　　　(Student repeats.)

Teacher model: /popopopo/
　　(Student repeats.)
Teacher model: /opo/
　　(Student repeats.)
Teacher model: /up, up, up/
　　(Student repeats.)
Teacher model: /af/
　　(Student repeats.)
Teacher model: /fufufufu/
　　(Student repeats.)
Teacher model: /af af af/
　　(Student repeats.)

Mark the consonant sound in the appropriate column, remembering to listen *only* for the consonant production. Continue modeling this way until two or three consonant sounds have been written in the Phonetic column. You do not need to assess all of the consonants; stop when two or three goals have been identified.

# Summary

This chapter explained the importance of finding time for a good speech production evaluation. We noted that a thorough evaluation is critical to the development of an appropriate spoken communication program. We also noted that any member of the team could administer the suggested evaluation instruments.

Two types of evaluations were described. An Oral Peripheral Exam, which assesses a child's oral-motor speech abilities, was provided with the appropriate instructions. The Student Speech Record (SSR), a new easy-to-administer speech production checklist, was also described and an example SSR dialogue presented. Within the context of the SSR, three instructional levels were identified: phonetic, phonologic, and pragmatic.

After reviewing the results of the two evaluations, the team members can easily determine where to begin spoken communication instruction, which objectives are most appropriate, and the level at which the training should begin.

# Chapter 6 Topics for Discussion

1.  Explain the importance of completing an Oral Peripheral Exam prior to initiating speech work in the classroom.

2.  If a child has a difficult time coordinating tongue movements, what sort of diagnostic indicator might that be in regards to speech production?

3.  Name and describe the four components of speech communication as listed on the Student Speech Record.

4.  Explain the purpose of dividing speech into the phonetic, phonologic, and pragmatic production categories.

5.  Following the administration of an Oral Peripheral Exam and the Student Speech Record, can you think of a situation where speech production might never be an appropriate objective for a student?

# Chapter 7

# Learning Styles

In the previous chapters we discussed making your classroom a communication-friendly one, and how to begin your spoken communication program by evaluating the students' existing skills. The next step is to review various learning styles so that we can better implement new strategies into our teaching.

> The Johnson family recently purchased a new entertainment center for their family room, and it was just delivered on Saturday morning. In their excitement, the family members all wanted to set up their new toy. Ben, the father, called his friend who had recently set up his own center to come and explain how to put it together. Barbara, the mother, immediately took out the instruction manual and began to read the directions. Mark, their sixteen-year-old son, started unwrapping the cords, examining the buttons and outlets, and plugging things in.

As individuals, we all have our favored learning styles. Ben prefers to hear the information explained to him, because he processes auditory input more efficiently. Barbara likes to read the new information because she is a visual learner and prefers to see the directions. Mark is a tactile/kinesthetic learner who prefers to use his hands to learn. Some of these traits are inborn, and others are learned as we grow. Recent research shows that all children are "wired" differently at birth (Levine, 2002). It is how we nurture the child's traits in our teaching that will result in success or frustration for the learner. It is important to remember that it is not significant *how* we process the information as long as the new knowledge *is*, indeed, processed.

# How a Multisensory Approach Complements Learning Styles

Most classes in which we find deaf children are not homogeneous but rather, include students with mild-moderate, severe, and profound hearing losses. Using a multisensory approach to teaching will provide students with a broader spectrum from which to acquire their knowledge, regardless of their preferred learning styles. Instead of painting with a broad brush and seeing all class members as having the same learning styles, an insightful teacher recognizes students as unique individuals. Some students are good artists while others are strong readers; one child may be beautifully expressive and loves acting, while others like computers and technology. We suggest that these learning styles have so much in common that to use them *all* will improve your teaching and the effectiveness of instruction.

According to Stewart and Kluwin (2001), "Learning style is a flexible construct whose meaning can range from those people who are better at listening to information to those people who prefer to see information" (p. 283). Children are born with a dominant learning style and other styles can be acquired or trained as they grow (Levine, 2002).

Regardless of their level of hearing, students who are deaf obtain information using a variety of different strategies or learning styles. It is widely stated that vision plays a significant role in learning for deaf and hard of hearing children (Easterbrooks & Baker, 2002; Northern & Downs, 2001; Moores, 2001; Schirmer, 2001, 1994). The fact is that children with hearing loss are no different than any other children with regard to learning style. Even though ASL is a visual and gestural language, it is still a verbal language (Stewart & Kluwin, 2001). Children with hearing loss need the opportunity to learn spoken language from many sensory avenues. Clearly, the visual avenue is one that may be a rich source of stimulation for the child if she is a visual learner.

It seems obvious that students who are profoundly deaf will get their information *primarily* through the visual sense, but students who are hard of hearing also include audition as one mode through which learning takes place. Just as some students prefer to learn visually and others prefer their auditory sense, almost every learner welcomes the opportunity to actually *experience* the new information by touching and doing. In this chapter, we will examine specific historical strategies, that utilize all of these learning styles: visual, auditory, and tactile/kinesthetic.

# Learning Styles from a Historical Perspective

We can learn from our predecessors in deaf education, who utilized many strategies for teaching through the various learning modes. It is important to examine historical perspectives to understand how we can adapt these methods for use in today's classrooms. Although some strategies may appear outdated, we shouldn't discount them as a whole.

## Visual Strategies

The use of visual strategies to develop language began at the same time that deaf education was initiated in the 1500s. Initially, visual strategies were tied to written or manual language. Pedro Ponce de Leon (writing), Juan Pablo Bonet (manual signs and writing), and William Holder (writing and speechreading) all used written forms of language, breaking words and sentences into segments and then modeling the spoken form. Work focused on articulation of phonemes and syllabication.

Alexander Graham Bell introduced the **Speech Glove** and **Visible Speech** in the mid-1800s. These visual cueing systems gave the student a more specific referent for each speech sound. The use of the Speech Glove allowed the student to have a visual sense of tongue position within the mouth, providing a more tangible means of seeing where a sound was produced. This was an important addition to the previously limited visual strategies because it is possible to actually see only about one-third of all speech sounds.

As teachers of D/HH students continued to utilize the importance of the visual channel, more visual strategies developed. The **Fitzgerald Key** brought metalinguistic symbols to the attention of deaf educators. Marguerite Stoner used similar symbols extensively in the spoken communication program used initially by the John Tracy Clinic in the early 1900s. These symbols represented the suprasegmentals aspects of spoken language, as seen in Figure 7.1. A rise or fall in inflection had specific symbols. Syllabication, which

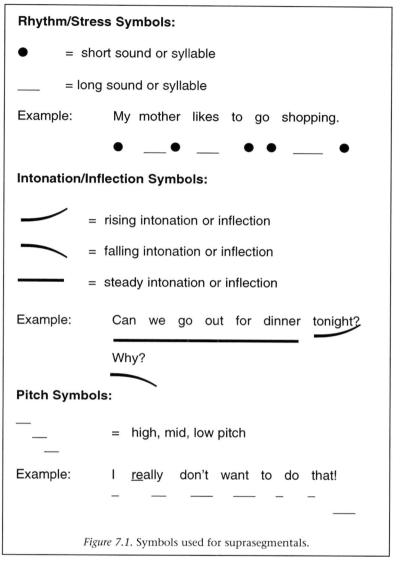

*Figure 7.1.* Symbols used for suprasegmentals.

is a component of speech rhythm, was easily noted with dots and dashes. Dictionary diacritics were used to show stressed and unstressed syllables. Students could easily see these meta-cues accompanying the written material and adjust their suprasegmental speech production using the cues.

Another written visual strategy was the **Association Method**. Mildred McGinnis originally developed this method in 1963, for children with aphasia. Its use with deaf and hard of hearing children was reserved for those students who had the greatest difficulty producing speech. Each sound is taught individually both through audition and in writing, is color-coded, and then coarticulated in print through the use of cursive writing. The student would say each sound, blending into the next sound as the letters were connected in writing. This was a tedious process and was rarely used by deaf educators.

A visual strategy that was developed over 40 years ago, and that is currently finding increased support, is **Cued Speech**. Cued Speech is a system developed by Dr. Orin Cornett in the mid-1960s. The system includes eight handshapes that represent the consonant sounds of English and five hand positions that represent the vowels (Figure 7.2). The original intent of Cued Speech was to help deaf

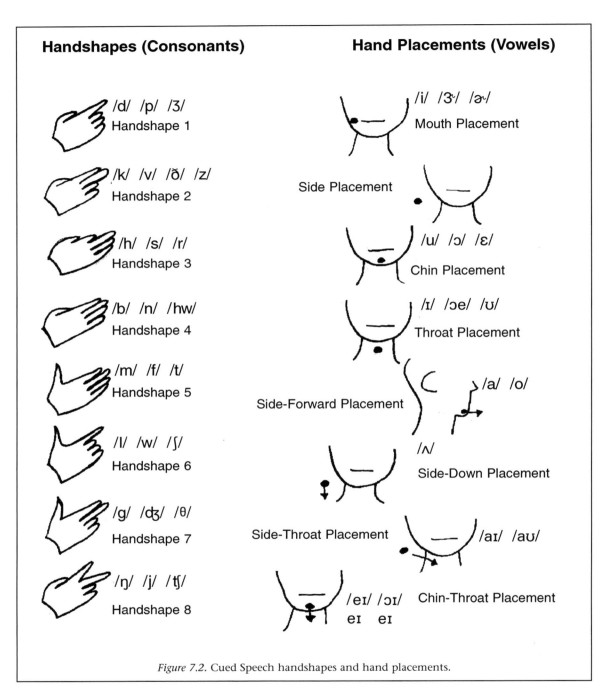

*Figure 7.2.* Cued Speech handshapes and hand placements.

children develop improved reading skills by providing them with a visual phonics system. This system has the potential to become a significant breakthrough in the use of visual strategies to develop spoken language and literacy.

Another recent visual program is the **Visual Phonics/See the Sound** program (International Communication Learning Institute [ICLI], 1988). Visual Phonics is a system of 46 hand cues and corresponding written symbols to facilitate development of speech as well as reading skills. These cues are used in conjunction with spoken language and represent individual sounds. The hand cues selected for Visual Phonics are in some ways suggestive of how the sounds are produced. These cues provide a concrete way for deaf and hard of hearing children to conceptualize how to produce a sound and then to see how that sound relates to its printed correlate (Marshall, Nussbaum, & Waddy-Smith, 1999).

The Visual Phonics system was developed by the mother of three deaf children who felt that there had to be a more visual way of representing the sounds of English. She created symbols and accompanying hand movements that match each of the English speech sounds. The program contains a series of classroom flash cards and posters along with other instructional materials. Each symbol is printed on a classroom flash card with the Standard English grapheme, Thorndike dictionary diacritics, and common written letter combinations. On the back of each card is a pronunciation statement and the description of how to represent the sound using handshapes and hand/arm movements.

Vanessa Wilson-Favors (2000), a speech therapist who worked with deaf students, used the Visual Phonics/See the Sound System and reported that her students "acquired the target sounds more rapidly than expected; the students performed better on their (speech) post-test; all six students showed progress in the correct articulation of their target sounds although in some cases progress was minimal." Wilson-Favors also noted that there was a need for a number of modifications to the program because of weaknesses relating to coarticulation and assimilation of speech sounds as well as allophonic variations that occur within speech that were not represented in the system.

The program materials are available from the International Communication Learning Institute. Anyone who wants to use the system must attend a six- to eight-hour training session by a licensed trainer before the materials can be purchased or used. The ICLI Company can be contacted for a list of certified trainers.

To summarize, historically, a number of programs or strategies have been used to stimulate the visual input mode for spoken communication. Each of these strategies has had proponents who adamantly believed in their efficacy. In fact, each strategy certainly worked for a number of children.

## Auditory Strategies

Historically, in deaf education, little attention was paid to teaching children auditorally, as this would have been seen as a waste of time. In fact, the entire concept of teaching deaf children by employing their residual hearing is relatively new. Goldstein, whose work extended between the 1890s and 1941, believed that by simply amplifying the sound with an ear trumpet, a deaf person could obtain information auditorally. He used mostly environmental sounds rather than encouraging the comprehension of spoken language. In the 1940s, the incorporation of speechreading, audition, and vibrotactile information made for a more multisensory approach. With a child's hearing aid and other methods of classroom amplification, deaf children were encouraged to use vision, audition, and tactile methods to learn in school. Many students with moderate hearing losses experienced success, but profoundly deaf children had less satisfactory results (Calvert & Silverman, 1983; Bunch, 1987; Moores, 2001).

In the 1960s and 1970s, advances were made in amplification with the miniaturization of hearing aids and the development of more high-powered aids. As cited in Bunch (1987), Pollack and Grammatico, Beebe, Pearson, and Koch were among those who believed in a unisensory approach. Using this method, students were encouraged to use only their auditory sense, and full mainstreaming into a regular classroom was the ultimate goal. The auditory-only approach was referred to, in the past, as the Auditory-Oral, Aural-Oral, Acoupedic, Unisensory-Auditory, Auditory-Verbal, and Acoustic methods (Calvert & Silverman, 1983).

All of these methods have many factors in common, and today they have merged under the common name of **Auditory-Verbal Method.**

The Auditory-Verbal approach is based upon a logical and critical set of guiding principles which enable children who are deaf or hard of hearing to learn to use even minimal amounts of amplified residual hearing or hearing through electrical stimulation (cochlear implants) to listen, to process verbal language, and to speak. It involves training the child to use even minimal amounts of residual hearing to develop spontaneous speech and to process language in a natural way through auditory pathways. (Auditory-Verbal International, Inc., 2000–2001)

*Using Music to Teach Speech.*    A number of educators and scientists have advocated using music to teach speech to children who are deaf or hard of hearing. Starting as early as the 1950s, professionals such as Sandberg, Guberina, Martinov, Edwards, Atkins, and Donovan (as cited in Parker & Koike, 1984) either taught music for music's sake or utilized music specifically to teach speech. Regardless of this philosophical difference, music can be a very useful tool for teaching various speech parameters. Through listening and singing, performing with instruments, and moving with music, the use of musical rhythms and melodies helps deaf children develop natural rhythm and intonation patterns of speech (Parker & Koike). Residual hearing is also explored through singing and listening since children must naturally pay attention to musical sounds, which are auditory. Most of the musical sounds are reported to be within the aided range of even some profoundly deaf children.

## Tactile and Kinesthetic Strategies

Tactile and kinesthetic strategies involve those activities that enable a student to use the external sense of touch or the internal sense of kinesthesia to modulate speech reception and production. As you read through the visual and auditory strategies, it is apparent that there is significant overlap among the four areas of learning. For instance, the Visual Phonics/See the Sound Program and Association Method clearly have a kinesthetic component.

In 1970, Anthony van Uden introduced a method of instruction called the **Maternal Reflexive Method.** Many of the strategies suggested by van Uden involved the tactile and kinesthetic senses. From using musical instruments and focusing on vibrations to incorporating the use of touch into speech activities, van Uden believed that a deaf child would have more access to speech if allowed to feel its components.

Dr. Petar Guberina, a linguist from Croatia, developed a system called the **Verbo-Tonal Method.** A primary focus of the Verbo-Tonal Method was the use of rhythm in the development of speech skills. Music, poetry and choreography were all components of the Verbo-Tonal Method. Another important component was the use of a SUVAG (System of Universal Verbotonal Audition Guberina) amplification unit. The SUVAG was unique because several students could be hooked up to the amplification device simultaneously, yet it was designed to meet the amplification needs of each user. The SUVAG could be set to specifically amplify the sounds that were a part of each student's optimal dynamic range of hearing. Kinesthesia was the primary teaching/learning component of the Verbo-Tonal Method. Children were trained to feel the difference between tense and relaxed speech sounds. This was accomplished through poetry, games, literacy activities, music, and choreographic activities. The Verbo-Tonal Method is still used across Europe and in some schools in the United States.

# Summary

We have discussed the four main learning styles by which human beings acquire knowledge of the world around them. Visual learners are those who prefer to gain information through sight; auditory learners prefer to learn through listening; and tactile/kinesthetic learners prefer to learn through touching and performing activities. Since learning styles are believed to be neuropsychological cognitive skills rather than completely sensory ones, students who are deaf use similar strategies to learn as their hearing peers. In other words, a visual learner does not see better than an auditory learner and an auditory learner does not have better hearing than the visual learner does.

Historically, we learned about strategies that were used in the past while keeping in mind how we can adapt these for use in our own specific teaching situations. In the following chapter, we will discuss strategies that are successful in present-day classrooms.

# Chapter 7 Topics for Discussion

1. Why does it make sense to view a child's spoken communication skills from a learning style perspective?

2. What do tactile and kinesthetic strategies have in common?

3. Define the learning problems a profoundly deaf child who is an auditory learner may encounter in a general education classroom.

4. Determine your own learning style by completing the learner style survey at the following web site: http://www.ldpride.net/learningstyles.MI.htm

# Chapter 8

# Teaching Strategies

Chapter 7 examined the four main learning styles used by most people to learn new information: visual, auditory, and tactile/kinesthetic. Now, we turn our focus to the strategies teachers can use to meet the needs of students who prefer these various styles. Teachers in different settings will agree that it is wise to vary one's teaching strategies because of the heterogeneous nature of classroom groupings. Students who are deaf or hard of hearing deserve the same diverse and exciting programs in their education as their hearing counterparts.

The key issue regarding the successful use of these strategies is that no single strategy works for every child. As we stated earlier, each child develops his own personal learning style. Within that style, one particular strategy may be more appealing and therefore more effective for that child. Also, using any single strategy with a child on a one-to-one basis rather than in a true communicative milieu inhibits the ability to communicate fluently in an interactive environment. Parents, speech therapists, and teachers must be knowledgeable about and comfortable in using multiple strategies in classroom or group situations.

As a teacher of any type, it is important to be multimodal; that is, able to utilize a variety of teaching strategies to meet the needs of the students. When you understand how children learn, you can help them develop ways to use their dominant style while helping to strengthen the weaker ones. We are not suggesting that one method is vastly better than another. We do suggest that in order for a student to become a well-equipped user of spoken communication, the team must create an overall classroom-learning environment that makes learning fun as well accessible to all types of learners. We are suggesting that some or all of these strategies may be used in any type of classroom setting. Regardless of whether the student is in a self-contained classroom, being tutored by a speech teacher, in an Auditory/Oral classroom, or in a bilingual classroom, the strategies suggested here may be modified to meet the needs of your teaching style and individual circumstances.

# Using Assessment Tools to Develop Instructional Strategies

Using the Student Speech Record as a guide, assess the spoken communication needs of the students in the class. There may be several common objectives among the students. Use those objectives to select a few activities that will enhance the spoken communication skills of all students in the class. For example, several students may have difficulty with intonation. Use the suprasegmental skill of intonation as a basis for both phonetic and phonologic practice activities.

In the following sections, we provide the reader with a series of instructional strategies written in a narrative form. The strategies are easy to follow, replicate, and adapt for your classroom.

# Visual Strategies

The following suggestions will be helpful not only to the D/HH child in the classroom, but to every child who has difficulty with spoken communication skills. In each section you will find a description of a strategy and a discussion of its use in the classroom.

## Using the International Phonetic Alphabet

Children love to speak and write in code. The International Phonetic Alphabet (IPA) (see Figure 6.3, page 65) is a visual code that has symbols representing all of the English speech sounds. Aside from a few very different-looking symbols, most of the sounds in the IPA are represented by English graphemes that children already know. Children do not have to learn an entire set of new symbols or pictographs, nor do they have to memorize special body movements that are specifically tied to any single speech sound.

In terms of teamwork, every speech therapist knows the IPA, most teachers of deaf and hard of hearing children have been exposed to the IPA as part of their course of study, and parents can learn to use it in a very short period of time. Children will learn it quickly because they will view it as a code and they will find that by using the IPA, they can more easily pronounce words that they have trouble decoding. IPA then, acts as a means of enhancing both spoken and written literacy skills.

## IPA Activities

The classroom is a place for discovery and the IPA can be used as a tool for discovering how words can be decoded. The following activities enable students to communicate with one another in a fun and stress-free manner, developing spoken language and written literacy skills along the way.

 **Spy Guy**

- Each day, once a week, or whenever the teacher chooses, a child in the class is selected to complete the task of being the Spy Guy. The Spy Guy assignment is a secret assignment.
- The teacher writes a note using IPA symbols (as needed) to the assigned Spy, who then reports to the teacher, reads the note aloud, and acknowledges the Spy Guy job. See Figure 8.1 for an example of such a note.

Dear Spy Guy,

Today I want you to try to camouflage /kæ mə flaʒ/ yourself when you see or hear me make a mistake in math. /ʃ/ It'll be our secret! Come tell me what this note says ☺!

*Figure 8.1.* Note written for Spy Guy.

- The Spy Guy's job is to watch and listen for the teacher's *communication errors* during a designated time period.
- The teacher uses a secret cue to indicate the time. Errors in communication may be either auditory or visual in form.
- The Spy Guy writes down the teacher's errors.
- At the end of the day, during a wrap-up activity, the Spy Guy reveals himself and *all* of the children help the teacher correct the identified errors.

 **Challenge**

- The children are divided into three teams with designated colors.
- The teacher writes vocabulary words on self-stick notes that match each group's color and hides them throughout the classroom.
- Each group has three minutes to go on a vocabulary scavenger hunt in the classroom.
- As a group, they must decide how to say each of the vocabulary words. Each group may use dictionary and IPA symbols to help each other pronounce the words.
- After five minutes, each group must take turns saying their new words.
- Anyone from another team can challenge the way the word is pronounced.
- If the speaker is saying the word correctly, his team earns a point. If a challenge is successful, the challenging team earns the point.
- The team with the most points wins the Challenge Cup for the day.

**I Say–You Say**

- This is a debate-style activity. The children work in teams of two to argue a side of a discussion.
- To make sure they are saying the words correctly, teams use IPA in their speech-writing efforts for their opening and closing statements.
- This is a particularly good strategy to incorporate crosscurricular information or thematic units.

 **Mighty Messenger**

- Each day, a different student is assigned the task of classroom messenger.
- The Mighty Messenger delivers any and all messages throughout the school or within the class.
- Messages are written using IPA when necessary and delivered through spoken language.
- When using this strategy outside of the classroom, it is critical for the other members of the school community to work collaboratively with you and your students. The school secretary, nurse, librarian, lunchroom assistant, and so on should be aware that part of your classroom activity is the job of Mighty Messenger. In that way, when your messenger arrives, the listener is more attentive and can appropriately reinforce the child's efforts.

## Activities for Older Students

Using the IPA is particularly effective with older students. How many times does a student ask how to pronounce an unfamiliar word? Typically we respond by stating the word or by telling the student to go look it up in the dictionary. Instead, write the word out using the IPA and have the student decode it for himself. See Figure 8.2. for sample high school level words written out using IPA.

Using the IPA to stimulate speech production is a visual, auditory, and kinesthetic strategy. Students see the difference in written sounds, listen for the differences when charged to do so, and practice production by monitoring oral decoding skills.

| Use the IPA symbols to help you read and say these words correctly. | |
| --- | --- |
| Parachute | ch = /ʃ/ |
| Tranquility | tr = /tʃr/ |
| Oedipal | Oe = /ɛ/ |
| Gnarl | gn = /n/ |
| Undulate | du = /dʒə/ |
| Yacht | ach = /ɑ/ |
| Yeoman | eo = /o/ |
| Petulant | tu = /tʃu/ |

*Figure 8.2.* Sample high school level words written out using IPA.

# Auditory Strategies

## Ensuring Successful Listening

It is vitally important that teachers have success in mind for auditory learning to take place. As Louise Tracy reminds us in the foreword to the book *Play It by Ear* (Lowell & Stoner, 1960), we must ". . . bring about understanding, incentive, and know-how, as well as . . . acceptance of auditory limitations, and a realization that this is but one approach to be used and not abused, and to be fitted into a total program."

The use of auditory strategies should not be viewed as a game of Stump the Student, but as simple activities to *reinforce* previously learned concepts and communication skills. Never give a student a challenge that you know he cannot do. This will surely cause frustration and disappointment. We do not want the student to perceive himself as a failure. All of the following suggestions can be tried auditorally *if* the teacher believes that the child will positively benefit from the activity by learning to discriminate and comprehend various spoken English patterns.

## Creating Auditory Lessons

A skilled teacher of deaf children will use a variety of strategies when planning daily lessons. Objectives should be stated clearly, using specific language that explains how they will be met. By including objectives such as "The child will: read, write, participate in, listen to, act out," and so on, the teacher can add specific strategies that enhance auditory learning.  During the lesson and upon its completion, teachers should check for understanding by asking relevant questions to evaluate the students' knowledge. In anticipation, write a list of possible questions that you will want to include and then add two or three aimed at auditory awareness. Always select your questions carefully, with a positive outcome in mind: that the student will surely succeed. In nearly every lesson, there can be opportunities to listen and practice some form of auditory skill.

Suggested here, you will find three categories of ways to incorporate auditory strategies into your classroom or tutoring session: music, poetry and choral readings, and phonemic awareness.

## Music

Many songs can be used to teach the prosodic aspects of speech, but a favorite of young students is one called *When I Sing La La La* (Brady, 1977). This song emphasizes the students' ability to practice the suprasegmental aspects of speech without having to concentrate on learning new words. The song leader varies the intonation, intensity, and duration of his voice while the children listen to these vocal changes and then repeat each line of the song. Most songs written for hearing children can be used with children who are deaf or hard of hearing as well. The sheet music for this song and the website where other fun children's songs may be found is in Appendix E.

Some songs are specifically written to help children learn new phonetic sounds for reading.  For example, students enjoy this song, which helps them practice saying the /p/ sound:

> *I have a pink pig,*
> *A pretty, pink pig,*
> *A pretty pink pig you see.*
> *When I pet my pig,*
> *My pretty pink pig,*
> *Some pennies come out for me!*

The students take pleasure from singing since there is no requirement for performance, only for participation, and they are learning about rhythm and intonation while practicing the sound /p/.

Other songs can be learned that aid in the memorization of new material or linguistic patterns. If the words from commercially made materials are too advanced or too juvenile, adapt them to your classroom needs. The musical selections for typical lessons are endless as a teacher considers the many topics to cover in a day. Songs can be sung as part of memorizing days of the week, months of the year, counting by tens, fives, and so on.

***For Older Students.*** It is important to capitalize on a student's interest, and there is little that is more interesting to an adolescent than music. Even students who are deaf or hard of hearing connect with the rhythms of their generation's musical genres. Use the rhythm of their music to stimulate speech production within the academic content areas. Have your students write a rap song for history class:

> *Yo, yo, JFK, fought his way, through the waves*
> *On his boat, that was fine, think it's called PT 109.*

a ballad for English:

> *Shakespeare, Shakespeare was a lark,*
> *Always wrote about love that was dark.*

a folk song for science:

> *Where have all the test tubes gone?*
> *Long time autoclaved.*
> *Where have all the amoebas gone?*
> *Meiosis knows. . . .*

By using music and rhythm as a stimulus, you encourage accurate production of suprasegmental speech components as well as enable the monitoring of accurate speech production. And it is fun!

***Rhythm Games.*** At math time, elementary school teachers know the value of understanding patterns. Being able to predict what will "come next" is vital in making mathematical connections. By incorporating rhythm into the math lesson, the teacher provides the students another tool to aid in learning.

 **Rhythms**

- Sitting cross-legged in a circle, have the students follow your pattern as you pat your knees and clap your  hands.
- Add a snap into the pattern, as students become more comfortable with the rhythm.
- Introduce a vocal pattern with the beat: (patting knees = red, red, red), (clapping hands = blue).
- Practice the pattern together as a group—(red, red, red, blue)—until the students' natural rhythm takes hold.
- Take turns with the students creating new patterns and increasing the length to make the rhythmic pattern more challenging.

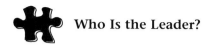 **Who Is the Leader?**

- A fun game related to Rhythms is called "Who Is the Leader?"
- Send one student out of the room for a moment.
- The remaining students decide on who will serve as the pattern leader.
- The leader then begins a pattern and all of the others follow his lead. He may change patterns at any time, and all the others should follow without making it obvious who they are following.
- When the student reenters the room, he watches to see if he can tell who the leader is and makes his guess.
- This game can be modified by adding words to the patterns.

## Poetry and Choral Readings

Although related to music, learning poetry and performing choral readings are different ways of incorporating the listening sense into your classroom. Simple nursery rhymes, fingerplays, and other forms of poetry encourage the children to use and strengthen their auditory memory and spoken communication skills. Students enjoy poems relating to thematic teaching units, and the repetitive and predictable nature of poetry lends itself toward easy memorization. Schimmel, Edwards, and Prickett (1999) note that a sense of auditory memory is an important aspect in learning to read new words and predicting English sentence patterns.

If you are unable to find poetry or rhymes that match your objectives, you can always create your own choral readings to fit the needs of your classroom. When teaching a unit on Halloween, you may make up a story such as the one below.

> *The witch says, "Ee-ee-ee!"*
> *The owl says, "Whooooo?"*
> *The ghost says, "BOOO!"*
> *The black cat says, "Meeeow."*
> *The monster says, "Aaaggh!"*

As the students grow comfortable with choral reading and begin to recognize the sounds in your story, they get speech practice in a fun context without any drill work or pressure. Even the youngest students are capable of learning to memorize and appreciate poetry. The students particularly enjoy learning a poem and practicing the lines together as a group.

Several strategies can be used to learn to recite poetry individually or as a group. The printed text can be presented before it is memorized (visual strategy) or after it is already memorized. Visual learners will prefer to see the poem first and then memorize later. Auditory learners will like to hear it first and then say it to themselves as they memorize. Both methods will be successful and will result in helping children to read and develop their auditory memory and spoken communication skills.

A number of classic books of poetry are available in commercial bookstores. Shel Silverstein, a well-liked author of poetry for children, wrote poems that are often humorous and highly motivating for children of all ages. His books, among many others, create a stepping-stone to using poetry to improve speech production.

## Phonemic Awareness

Many teachers of deaf children do not expect their students to succeed in reading using a phonemic approach to learning new words. However, learning to read by memorizing all of the words in the English language by sight alone would be an impossible task. There are many successful D/HH readers who have a sense of phonemic awareness, although it is unknown exactly how it is acquired (Schimmel et al., 1999). Skilled deaf readers make use of phonological information more often than average deaf readers (Hanson, Goodall, Perfetti, Kelly, Schaper, & Reitsma, as cited in Schimmel et al.). Whether deaf or hearing, multiple tools are used to develop adult-level reading skills. We believe that by providing every student the opportunity to have experiences with phonemic awareness, his chances for success in reading and using spoken communication may be increased. In the following section, we suggest activities that support practice of spoken communication while also making use of teachable moments in reading and writing the English language.

 **Experience Charts**

The classroom teacher uses Experience Charts in many ways. Generally, these charts are written accounts of a story or experience that the teacher wants to share with the students. Depending on the age and abilities of the students, experience charts can be very simple or quite sophisticated. The most successful experience charts are those that are student-generated, because the students' own ideas are shown in writing. As a tool for teaching language, experience charts are invaluable. To take them and use them to help foster reading, writing, vocabulary, speech, and listening is to use them to an even greater magnitude.  Look at the many possibilities resulting from the experience chart activity that follows:

- The teacher and first grade students have just shared a learning experience hiding a ball in various locations around the room. Each child had a turn to hide the ball <u>under</u> the chair, <u>behind</u> the door, <u>on</u> the counter, and so on.
- The teacher prepares an experience chart to enable the children to learn a specific sentence pattern as they describe the action taken.
- The pattern of the chart may look something like this:
    *Sally put the ball under the chair.*
    *Robert put the ball on the counter.*
    *Jose put the ball behind the door.*
- To take the lesson to the next level, the teacher should ask each student to take a marker and underline certain words, depending on the objectives of the lesson.
- He asks one student to underline all of the proper names in one color or each of the prepositions in another.
- He asks, "Where did Robert put the ball?" to check for understanding of prepositions.
- The teacher asks another student to find all of the words that begin with the sound /b/ and another to identify all of the words that begin with the sound /p/.
- A quick lesson is at hand and students should notice that the letters *b* and *p* are very similar in how they are produced.
- The teacher asks who can describe the difference between the two sounds. The students will learn that although both sounds are produced in the same manner and have the same placement, one has voice and one does not.

- As the teacher places a tissue in front of his lips, the students see that a puff of air comes out with the sound /p/, but the tissue barely moves with production of the /b/.
- Using the experience chart, the teacher asks the students to "listen and find" the sentence that he says. Keeping a successful outcome in mind, he asks who wants to find the sentence that says, "Jose put the ball behind the door"?

While working on language experience activities, remember to keep a closed set of options by saying, "I will say this sentence or this sentence" as you point to each. This narrows the student choices and facilitates the activity. Keeping in mind the students' individual capabilities, be sure that you select goals that are within reach for all of the students.

 **Secret Word**

- At the beginning of the day, the teacher selects a new vocabulary word that will be the secret word of the day. This may be a new vocabulary word or just a fun word chosen by one of the students.
- With each transition time during the day, the teacher gives directions and then gives the "green light" by saying the secret word.
- For example, after the math lesson, the teachers says, "Now get your books, turn to page twelve, and sit down at your desks (pause) Popcorn." Then the children know that the teacher has completed giving the directions and they can continue.

 **Secret Sound**

In a similar way, a new sound can be introduced at the beginning of the week. This can be a sound that will be learned in reading and can be reinforced at all times of the day.
- If, for example, the sound to be learned is /f/, the teacher would introduce this at the beginning of the week.
- At reading time, students may learn that it may be spelled *f* as in *four* or *ff* as in *off* or *ph* as in *phone.*
- At math time, they may notice the number words that have the /f/ sound in them.
- Depending on the age of the students, they may discover how the sound is produced, what it looks like to see it on the lips, how to fingerspell it, and how to write the letter *f.*
- As they progress through their day, each time the children correctly identify a new word containing the /f/ sound, they are given a point.
- Extra credit points may be earned for children out at recess who notice a new word with the /f/ sound.

# Tactile/Kinesthetic Strategies

To assure that the learning styles of all children are addressed, teachers and parents should also use tactile and kinesthetic strategies in teaching spoken communication, in addition to the visual and auditory tactics previously discussed. By definition, the word *tactile* refers to the sense of touch and *kinesthesia* refers to movement. Since these two are closely related, the strategies will seem connected and there may be a great deal of overlap in activities. Besides being useful teaching tools, tactile and kinesthetic strategies are fun!  And when learning is fun, it beomes more firmly embedded in one's repertoire.

As young children, we learn by feeling, touching, doing, and experiencing. You could hardly expect a preschooler to learn about the world around him through a discussion and lecture model of education. But interestingly, as we get older, our brains still like to learn from having first-hand experience with new information.

## Tutoring Time

When we are tutoring a child in spoken communication, as is the case in pullout speech therapy or direct instruction center-time, we have only a short amount of time to achieve our objectives. To make the best use of this time, break up the session into segments of phonetic learning and phonologic practice.

A well-prepared speech teacher will have a speech box with many tactile/kinesthetic materials available at his disposal. Suggestions for the speech box include, but are not limited to:

> Tissues
> Large candle that can stand on its own
> Birthday candles
> Lighter
> Bubbles
> Balloons
> Feathers
> Pictures of common words containing specific sounds
> Letter cards
> Blank cards and markers
> Chalk
> Rubber bands
> Candy sprinkles
> Cotton balls

Some of these items can help the teacher demonstrate what happens to speech sounds as they are emitted. Try some of the suggestions below.

- Use popcorn. Line up the pieces along your forearm and try to blow them off using the /p/ sound.  Like ducks at the shooting gallery, the popcorn pieces will blow off as each successful /p/ is produced.

- Feathers are convenient to use with the /f/ sound, for two reasons. One is that the word *feather* begins with the sound /f/, and the other is that feathers' lightweight nature shows movement when blown. Students can blow a feather on a pre-made game board, off of a sleeve, or along a desk. The word *off* is useful since the student is blowing the feather *off* of something as well as producing the /f/ sound.

- Candles are useful tools for showing breath stream. The easiest way to keep from relighting the candle each time is to light a large candle that can stand on its own and then use birthday candles for the actual activity. Holding the birthday candle in front of your lips, say the sound /pa/ or any other plosive sound as you blow out the flame.

- Use the candle strategy for fricative sounds as well. When producing an /f/, /s/, or /h/, the candle will flicker for the duration of the breath stream, but should not blow out.
- Bubbles are a fun and reinforcing way to practice breath support. Although it seems simple, very young children, both hearing and deaf, find it difficult to control and direct their breath stream. By showing a gentle but controlled breath stream, bubble-blowing activities allow children to feel and see the results of their controlled breath stream, and the activities are fun as well.

## "No Materials Needed"

Not all tactile or kinesthetic strategies require special materials. Many strategies utilize things that are readily available. In the past, it was not unusual for teachers to use a child's hands or fingers to point out or control the articulation of some sounds. For example, the teacher might have used a finger to push the tip of a child's tongue up to the alveolar ridge to produce a /t/ sound. This kind of intrusive activity is not only unhealthy, but also unnecessary. Some forms of touch are appropriate and helpful, but in all cases, good judgment and discretion should prevail when using any form of physical tactile prompt. Some appropriate prop-free tactile strategies are suggested below.

- A gentle touch on the cheek or the side of the nose helps to show the nasal characteristic of the "m," "n," and "ng" sounds. It can also help a child to monitor hypernasal speech production.
- The teacher tells the student to lick his forefinger and hold it in front of his lips. He tells him to feel the air as he says /f/.
- To show voicing on a sound, the teacher tells the student to gently hold his hand against his cheek or the larynx.
- The teacher directs the students to say the sound /tʃ/ to themselves several times. Now have students close their eyes and say it again. Have them notice how they pay more attention to the placement of their tongue, how it gently touches the alveolar ridge for the /t/ before releasing the air for the /ʃ/. This is a good strategy for *reinforcing* the /tʃ/ sound.
- Using two round, blank stickers, the teacher writes the sounds for two speech sounds that he is targeting, for example, /a/ and /u/. He places the stickers on the child's hands, with the /a/ sound on the back of his left hand and the /u/ sticker on the back of his right. The child says the sound as the teacher points to each one. Have the student practice alternating /a-u-a-u/ until the sound becomes a new one: /w/. This strategy works for many sounds: /i-a/ becomes /j/ and /ta-s-ta-s/ becomes the blend /st/.

## For Older Students

It may seem that tactile/kinesthetic strategies are intended only for very young children. However, as adults, we use them every day in our spoken language. When we experience a slip of the tongue, not only are we using auditory feedback, but kinesthetic feedback as well. We know that what we said just did not feel right. We can encourage older students to use their own feedback mechanisms to monitor their speech production.

- The use of tongue twisters is an excellent way to train a student to monitor himself kinesthetically for verbal miscues. "She sells seashells by the seashore," "Peter Piper picked a peck of pickled peppers," and "How much wood would a woodchuck chuck if a woodchuck could chuck wood" are all familiar tongue twisters that can help a student learn to focus on the accurate production of targeted speech sounds. To enhance language as well as spoken communication, have the student write his own tongue twisters.

■ The use of contrastive word pairs also encourages the use of kinesthetic feedback and monitoring. Write word pairs on a sheet of paper or index cards, and have the student say each pair accurately as quickly as possible. The words should sound or feel nearly identical except for a single phoneme; that provides the contrast. Use this activity as an elocution contest in the classroom to encourage all students to articulate clearly. Sample word pairs might include: sharp-harp; match-man; picture-pitcher; engine-ensign.

Use the older student's ability to think through and self-monitor kinesthetic cues to encourage and reinforce more accurate spoken communication skills.

# Using the Strategies in Daily Lessons

Visual, auditory, tactile, and kinesthetic strategies are easily put to use in daily classroom activities. After any new material is presented visually or auditorally, using some sort of action practices the skill. Sometimes, this means reinforcing a math concept by demonstration, doing a group activity, or completing written work. Science is always understood better when the students perform experiments rather than just read a chapter in a book. Likewise, spoken communication skills can be taken to the next level by practice—by students using what they have learned in actual situations that carry meaning for them.

 **Warm-Up**

As students sit at a small table with the teacher, assign the left hand to be one sound, such as /a/, and the right hand to a different sound, such as /u/. As one hand hits the table, the students say that sound and as the other hand hits the table, they say the second sound. All sounds that have been learned during phonetic teaching can be used for this simple, 30-second, warm-up activity. When you have finished your warm-up, the regular lesson may begin.

 **Throw the Dice**

Make a cube with a letter of a known sound on each side, for instance, /s/, /m/, /p/, /t/, /f/, /a/. (A die has six sides.) Before beginning a reading lesson, the children take turns rolling the die and saying words that begin with each sound.

 **Write a Play**

The teacher can write a short play for the students to perform for parents, or one that can be videotaped for the class as a future teaching tool. The students' finest strengths can be assured by writing the lines that you know the children can say with confidence. The students can practice at home and at school until they feel comfortable with their roles.

 **Playtime**

When students are outside playing, the speech teacher may reinforce simple sounds such as "Wheeee" as they go down the slide. On the swings, he may model, "Uuuup and down" as the child moves back and forth. If something falls down, such as a stack of blocks, he may model, "Uh-oh" or imitate the sound of crashing blocks.

 **Guess the Letter**

In the reading lesson, after new letters and sounds are taught, play a guessing game that reinforces handwriting and letter-sound recognition. Have one student come up and turn his back to you while you "write" a letter on his back using your finger. See if the child can guess what letter you wrote and if he can say the sound. Have the children do this with partners as well.

 **Feelie Bags**

Place several objects that begin with a specially selected speech sound in a bag. Each child gets a turn to come up, feel in the bag, and blindly choose an object. When he pulls the object out of the bag, he can name it and use the word in a sentence.

 **Collage**

Students love to do art activities, so why not develop a lesson that is an art project and enhances speech development at the same time? Have the students find or draw pictures of things that begin with a designated sound. Have them show off their work by describing each picture. This could be a group activity as well: have the students break into teams, with each representing a different speech sound.

 **Fingerpainting**

During art time, let the children explore their artistic abilities by fingerpainting. As an extra speech activity, dictate certain sounds for which the students may write the matching letters. For instance, the teacher says, "Write the letter for the sound /fffffff/," and the children write with their fingers the letter *f*.

# Putting It All Together

We have provided a starting point with regard to the multiple opportunities that await teachers who wish to expand their repertoire of classroom-based spoken communication strategies. You will see these opportunities arise in your individual teaching situations and be able to extend and adapt them to fit your needs.

Spoken communication is a broad continuum of skills ranging from the basic structures of individual phonemes to the comfortable use of functional spoken English. Some students will come to be at ease with their use of speech, while others will utilize their skills only in certain circumstances. All students deserve the chance to reach their greatest potential for all forms of communication with a wider selection of people.

In Chapter 6, Evaluation, we discussed the three levels of speech production—phonetic, phonologic, and pragmatic. The simple progression from individual sounds to words and phrases that have meaning for the child can be likened to the progression from individual letters to the printed words, which become sentences and then paragraphs, chapters, and stories (Figure 8.3). Just as you wouldn't think of teaching only the letters of the alphabet and never the words and phrases that become the exciting stories of the printed word, neither would you teach speech sounds in isolation without ever giving those sounds meaning for the student.

Although the following example is too much for one lesson, it shows a natural progression and how you can take one simple sound with no meaning along the continuum to higher learning.

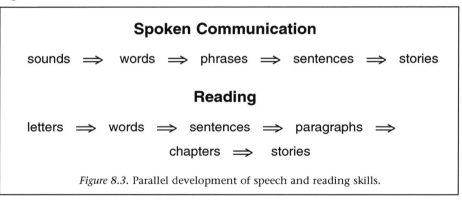

*Figure 8.3.* Parallel development of speech and reading skills.

**Not-So-Hypothetical**

Mrs. Foster is preparing her deaf and hard of hearing students for a lesson about the field trip the following day. The first graders are seated on the floor in a semicircle at the front of the room. "First, let's say that your left hand says, 'Oooo' and your right hand says, 'Aaaa.'" When Mrs. Foster and her students put their left hands on their left knees, they all say, "Ooo," and when their right hands go on their right knees, they say, "Aaa." She models slowly at first: left, right, left, right as they say, "Ooo-aaa-ooo-aaa." She then models faster and faster until the two sounds merge, forming the new sound "wa." Mrs. Foster explains that they have all just made the sound /w/. The students fingerspell the letter and "skywrite" it in the air. Some students come up to write the letter on the board.

"Now, let's brainstorm some words that begin with the /w/ sound." The list of words grows as the children sign their ideas: we, water, walk, will, want, and so on.

Refocusing on the task at hand—preparing for tomorrow's field trip to the museum—Mrs. Foster prepares a chart. "Where are we going tomorrow?" As the students answer each

*cont.*

question, she shows the students how to put their answers into sentences in written English. The student-generated story looks something like this:

*Tomorrow, we will go to the museum.*
*We will ride a bus.*
*We will see fossils and dinosaur bones.*

Mrs. Foster asks if the students notice any *w* words in their story and the children identify them. She teaches how the word *will* indicates future tense and that they have not yet completed this field trip. As an added lesson, a lesson on past tense can be taught after the field trip, noticing words such as *went, was,* and *were.*

Students of different ages, interests, and abilities will benefit from this sequence of showing how the English language works. The focus in this lesson was not the accurate speech production of the sounds, but rather the incorporation of a targeted sound into a functional communication milieu. Some students will actively participate with the spoken aspect of the lesson, and others will benefit by receiving the exposure and understanding a new concept.

# Summary

In this chapter, we described a variety of strategies for teaching spoken communication using four different learning styles: auditory, visual, and tactile/kinesthetic. It is recognized that all learners are "wired differently" and need different strategies to meet the wide array of individual learning styles (Levine, 2002). Human beings obtain information through hearing, sight, touch, and movement as they learn about the world around them. Deaf children are no different and will benefit from a variety of teaching strategies when learning spoken communication.

# Chapter 8 Topics for Discussion

1. Why is it important that we evaluate a student's learning style?

2. What is meant by the statement "All children are wired differently"?

3. Identify and describe the four basic learning styles.

4. Select one learning style and design a classroom-based activity for a child who is severely hard of hearing and has difficulties with all fricative sounds.

5. Using the sound /k/ as a target, design a classroom-based activity that would encompass all four learning styles.

6. Break into groups; then, using the materials in the speech box, take a targeted speech sound and create a series of activities for a breath control activity, suprasegmentals activity, phonetic level activity, phonologic level activity, and finally, a pragmatic level activity.

# Chapter 9

---

# Parents as Partners

Parents are one of the most important members of the multidisciplinary team. As teachers, we can never underestimate the value of the parents' opinions. They know their child, and have key information about their child's history, home life, her strengths and learning challenges, and how she will learn best. We must remember that we have our students for only six hours a day at most. Parents can and will make the difference in their interactions with their child for the other eighteen hours of the day. History shows us the impact that parental input has on the educational success of a child.

## Historical Overview of Parent Involvement in Education

In the early history of the United States, parents saw the need for schools. They raised the money, hired the teachers, formed the school boards, and fought for the rights of their children. In the education of deaf children, parents held a vital role in demanding the best educational programs for their children. As the years progressed, schools became less reliant on parents and became more driven by teachers and administrators (Kroth,1975). Over the course of time, deaf education and general education programs followed a similar path: parents placed the primary responsibilities for teaching their children with the schools and removed themselves from the instructional picture.

In more recent times, this trend continues; many parents work full-time and many teachers assume more responsibilities for the education of the student. When parents are less involved in the educational program, they are more likely to blame teachers and administrators for the perceived lack of progress in their children. When teachers are left with too much responsibility, they become more likely to blame parents for their perceived lack of interest in their own child.

Clearly, this "blame game" is not productive. No one wins when blame is the focus rather than the child. Too often, the educational process comes to a standstill when teachers and parents fault one another for a child's lack of progress. Parents have both the right and responsibility to question educational programs for their deaf children.

By working together as a team, parents and teachers eliminate these conflict-laden problems and work toward finding the solutions that are most likely to help the child succeed. A guiding principle for any multidisciplinary team effort is that parents and teachers have equal value on the team. Each one brings to the table a wealth of knowledge and concern. We must recognize one another's strengths and value one another's thoughts and insights into the child. When working in a positive manner with objectives clearly outlined, parents and teachers feel more satisfied—and more importantly, the child will have a greater likelihood of success.

# Chapter Focus

In this chapter, we will discuss different ways that parents can contribute to the multidisciplinary team and at varying levels of involvement. We will review the perceived roles and responsibilities of each team member, discuss opportunities for parents both at school and at home, and demonstrate some ideas that have been proven successful in programs for D/HH students throughout the country.

# Getting the Team Started

Call together a team meeting at the beginning of the school year. All team members should be invited and encouraged to attend. For this meeting, the team members should include the parents, the general education teachers, the teachers of deaf children, the student, and the speech and language pathologist. Begin by welcoming each team member. Once everyone is introduced, hand each member a copy of the Multidisciplinary Team Meeting Survey. (See Figure 9.1, and see Appendix F for reproducible form.) The purpose of this survey is to show each member her equal importance and value in the team effort. Notice that there is nothing on the survey that is negative; only positive comments are requested. Remind members to fill in all five areas of the form.

When the surveys are complete, have one person read the strengths of each team member as stated by the others. On a master sheet, jot down the roles and responsibilities listed by each team member, both as a future reference and to serve as a guide for the meeting. When team members understand their roles and their responsibilities, objectives can be identified and clearly understood.

---

**Multidisciplinary Team Survey**

As a valued team member, please fill out this survey. I would like to know how you rate the importance of each member of the team. I want _____ (student's name) to have the best year possible and I feel confident we can achieve this, if we all work together.

In what ways can the following team members contribute? Specifically, what can each person do? How do you see the strengths of these team members?

Classroom teacher:

Teacher of deaf and hard of hearing children:

Parent:

Student:

Speech Specialist:

*Figure 9.1.* Multidisciplinary Team Meeting Survey.

# Parents' Contributions

Parents can contribute in a variety of ways to their child's education, especially in the area of communication. Let parents know that *any* efforts made will be greatly appreciated. Understand that parents have a variety of reasons why they may *not* be able to participate in their child's education. Let us come up with reasons why they *can*.

Figure 9.2 is a parent form that can be distributed to parents at the beginning of the year. (Appendix F contains a reproducible version of this form.) This form was designed to be nonintimidating in that even five minutes a night is seen as a valuable contribution. Every classroom is different. Factors including grade level, teacher's presentation style, schedule, and ability to delegate responsibilities impact the types of parental activities offered. Modify this form as needed for your own classroom or teaching assignment. Giving a variety of options encourages parents to feel a part of their child's education, even if in a small way.

Before the parent fills out the sign-up sheet, discuss your policies regarding homework, centers, the Communication Book (see next section), parent communication, field trips, and other projects you have listed. Most parents will find at least one area in which they can help; others may see multiple volunteer opportunities. When parents come to volunteer in the classroom, they are showing their interest in supporting their child, the program in general, and you as the teacher. Parents demonstrate their priorities and feel important when they change their schedules to volunteer in the classroom.

> Dear Parents,
>
> I am so glad that you have agreed to be a partner in your child's education this year. There are many ways you can help. Please read the opportunities listed below and rank them in the order that you feel you can help.
>
> If you can commit to this on a regular basis, give it a **1**.
> If you can commit partially, give it a **2**.
> If you cannot commit to this, give it a **3**.
>
> _____ Help my child with homework
> _____ Work with my child four nights each week for ten minutes on the Communication Book
> _____ Come to the class to work in centers once a week for one hour
> _____ Come to the class to work in centers once a month for one hour
> _____ Participate in phone calling (as needed)
> _____ Volunteer on field trips
> _____ Help with bulletin boards
> _____ Help with special projects
> _____ Other ideas? Please explain. _____
> _____
>
> Do you have any special talents that you could share (art, music, storytelling, crafts, other?)
> _____
> _____
>
> Thank you for being a team member!
>
> Classroom Teacher_____
>
> Parent name, phone number, e-mail _____
> _____

*Figure 9.2.* Parents' contribution form for classroom participation.

On the parents' contribution form, there is an option that is unique to deaf education classrooms and specifically to the area of communication: the Communication Book. In addition, parents may volunteer in a special learning center called a communications center.

## Communication Books

Many teachers have tried developing a book that goes to and from school to help bridge the gap between home and school communication. Here, we will describe a way to merge the many communication book ideas we have seen used successfully in classrooms throughout the country. As you consider your own classroom needs, make modifications as needed. The Communication Book is one tried-and-true method that involves parents in helping their child practice communication skills.

Ask each child to bring in a three-ring binder, paper, and dividers. Give the students the time and materials to decorate their notebooks in a creative way. Each student must feel that the book is her personal creation and consequently will use it with pride. Pictures from home or school, artwork, and so on should be used to decorate the Communication Books. Have a lesson and accompanying activity entitled "What Is Communication?" to jumpstart the project. Once the book is prepared, decide on five areas on which to focus.

Generally, a Communication Book covers topics such as vocabulary, reading words, English sentence patterns, journalism, poetry, and spoken communication practice. Teachers of younger children often add subjects such as finger-plays or nursery rhymes. Teachers of older students may add topics such as social introductions, role-playing, or current events. The choice of Communication Book subjects may differ from classroom to classroom, but the goal remains the same: improve and enhance the students' communication skills and strategies.

After selecting the basic communication areas for the book, decide on individual goals for each section. The goals and objectives should match those noted in each child's IEP. Write these down and include them in the front of each student's book. Decide how often the students will work in the book, the length of time, and how often the book will go home. Some teachers may request that the book travel back and forth from school every day, as it may include specific homework assignments. Others may choose to have the books come to school once a week, when it is Communication Book day at the communications center.

Write directions for parents and include them in the front of the book. Be specific with what you would like the parent and the student to do. Do not put anything in the book that is difficult for the child or may cause stress between the student and his parent. The book should not be used for initial learning experiences, but rather for review and enrichment opportunities. The time spent working in the Communication Book should be a relaxing and enjoyable time between parent and child. See Appendix D for examples of Communication Book pages. Be creative with ideas and have a positive attitude toward all aspects of a child's communication.

***Communications Books for Secondary Students.*** Communication plays a key role in secondary students' lives. By this time, students have developed their primary mode of communication, be it sign or spoken English. Although some phonologic practice is still encouraged every day, *pragmatic* skills become more necessary at this time in a student's education.

The purpose of a secondary Communication Book is for students to practice skills necessary to communicate effectively with friends, family members, and strangers with whom they make contact routinely. It is important that students recognize this need for effective communication skills and show a commitment. Work in this book need not be considered a chore or a homework assignment to complete, but an opportunity to improve their spoken communication skills to ultimately enrich their lives. Several activities are included in Appendix D to help students and teachers get ideas for pragmatic practice.

## Communications Center: Involving Parent Volunteers

In Chapter 5, Creating a Speech-Friendly Classroom, we discussed the use of learning centers. This is an ideal way to work individually or in small groups in specific learning areas such as reading, writing, math, science, and communication. At the communications center, a wide variety of communication-related activities should be utilized. This is a worthwhile opportunity to practice previously learned skills, or to tutor students on individual spoken-communication objectives.

This is a perfect place for a parent volunteer! When parents come to help, make them feel welcome and comfortable; this is not their normal comfort zone. Introduce the parent as a team member in the class and give them the privilege to give praise or rewards for students who treat them with the respect they deserve.

Parent volunteers are wonderful teacher aides and usually feel more involved when they work directly with students, as integral parts of the class. Do not use parents to run copies or send them on errands taking them outside of the classroom. If you have parents come to volunteer during center time, encourage them to work at one of the centers. If the speech teacher will be tutoring at the communications center, the parent can update the Communication Book, practice sign language flash cards, review Communication Book pages, or practice any other skills previously learned in class. Figure 9.3 shows a checklist that can serve as a guide for teachers utilizing parents as classroom volunteers. A reproducible form of this checklist is available in Appendix F.

Ask parent volunteers to teach a specific skill to small groups or individuals. Give a written description for parents to follow when they arrive in the classroom. A simple step-by-step lesson plan will be most useful. After the parent has gained confidence and experience with her volunteering, you may find that she offers to develop these activities on her own.

---

**Teacher Checklist for Parent Volunteers**

When a parent agrees to become an active team member, be sure to ask yourself the following questions:

1. _____ Did you give the parent every opportunity to volunteer?

2. _____ Did you make the parent feel like a valued team member?

3. _____ Have you given the parent responsibilities with which he or she feels comfortable?

4. _____ When the parent comes to the classroom, will you introduce him or her as a team member?

5. _____ Do you have detailed plans for the parent volunteer to follow?

*Figure 9.3.* Teacher checklist for parent volunteers.

---

## Importance of Communication between Teacher and Parent

Communication between parents and teachers is vital to having a successful educational experience. Consider this example of a situation where the parent and teacher had a humorous communication breakdown:

---

**Not-So-Hypothetical**

Katie was a darling five-year-old, eager to begin her first day of kindergarten. She came to school dressed in her Sunday best, complete with a freshly ironed dress, clean white tights, and patent leather shoes. The teacher commented on how lovely the girl looked, but cautioned her to be careful on the playground.

On the second day, Katie came just as nicely dressed as on the first day. The teacher again complimented her nice outfit, but suggested she start wearing more casual clothing to school. Katie responded, "My mommy says I have to. She says I have to wear my pretty dress to school." The teacher could only wonder what this parent was thinking.

Every day of that first week, Katie came to school in a different dress, always clean and pressed and much too formal for school. On Friday after school, the teacher got a phone call from Katie's mother. The mother asked, "Is there some reason why Katie needs to wear such fancy clothes to school? Every day I ask her what she wants to wear to school, and she says, 'Mrs. Parker says I have to. Mrs. Parker says I have to wear my pretty dress to school.'"

Katie knew how to get what she wanted with her ability to communicate: to wear her pretty dress to school! Mrs. Parker and Katie's mom repaired their communication shortcomings and Katie, albeit a bit disappointed, wore more appropriate clothes to school from then on.

All team members are winners when they work and communicate as a team. With parental support, students will excel to their greatest ability. Without it, students may be forced to either make it on their own or possibly never realize their true potential.

# Summary

In this chapter we emphasized the need to include parents as equal partners in their children's efforts to develop spoken communication skills. We discussed two specific popular and effective strategies for encouraging parental participation—the Communication Book and communications center. Organizational suggestions were provided as well as several activities in which parents could easily assume leadership roles within their child's classroom. Finally, a survey, checklist, and parent information form were presented in the text and the appendices to assist the classroom teacher and speech and language pathologist in making the parent feel welcome as a fully contributing member of the child's spoken communication team.

# Chapter 9 Topics for Discussion

1. List at least five benefits to having parents working in the classroom with you.

2. Design a communications center activity that a parent can facilitate easily.

3. In addition to a daily Communication Book, what other means of communication are viable in either a classroom or itinerant educational setting?

4. Design a parent volunteer program for your educational setting.

# *Chapter 10*

# Using Technology to Enhance Spoken Language Development

Writing a chapter about using technology is like buying a new car: the minute you put pen to paper, the technology changes! Better yet, why talk about technology at all when discussing spoken language?

There are several important reasons for including a discussion about technology when focusing on the development and enhancement of spoken language skills. First and foremost is the point that technology is here to stay. The development of communication technologies has affected deaf and hard of hearing people tremendously. No longer must someone with a hearing loss be confined to the use of a sometimes-available TTY or the sometimes-convoluted use of a Relay Service. E-mail, listservs, and chatrooms bring easy communication to all people with hearing loss. As literacy skills improve, so does overall communication ability (French, 1999).

Another reason for discussing the use of technology is more pragmatic: children *love* to use technology. Not only are they enthralled with what they can control, but they also are reinforced for their skills and motivated to keep trying. They are *good* at it. As we have stressed throughout this book, it is critically important for the child to feel accomplished about the communication skills being developed. Technology is *fun!* When was the last time you remember any child feeling thrilled to work at any skill, let alone think that it is fun? In addition, a machine doesn't get irritated by repetition. A student can choose to repeat some element of a software application 100 times, and the computer won't grow bored or exhausted.

Technology has changed the face of speech work in all areas of the fields of speech and hearing. Both of these fields have come a long way from the days of working exclusively in front of a speech mirror. Today, a great variety of computer applications are specially designed for use with children who have some type of difficulty with spoken language communication.

This chapter will focus on both the computer systems (combined hardware and software) and software currently obtainable, recognizing that as we go to press, new and improved applications are becoming available. To facilitate the reader's ability to find these products, Appendices B and C include information about Internet websites and popular sources of technology hardware and software for people interested in developing or enhancing the speech and hearing skills of children with hearing loss.

# Computer Systems to Enhance Spoken Communication

Where would we be without computers today? IBM is a leader in the field when it comes to providing adaptable computer resources for individuals who have spoken language difficulties. With the introduction of the SpeechViewer, IBM brought the concept of biofeedback to the educational computer age. The SpeechViewer uses a box that is attached to the computer's CPU. Control knobs or switches on the box are used to modulate and adjust the various speech programs that are viewed on the monitor. A microphone plugs into the box so that the student's speech production can be viewed on the screen and be modified accordingly.

The SpeechViewer was one of the first computer-based products with a focus on the development and enhancement of spoken language skills through the use of visual and auditory feedback. Today, the SpeechViewer III's colorful and interactive programs encourage children to articulate sounds, modify vowel production, and modulate their vocal pitch and intensity. All of the modules in the SpeechViewer III software have games and other activities that allow the teacher to provide a visual and auditory model for a child. The child then has the opportunity to work individually or with partners to match the model or play the game. The focus of every game is a series of targeted speech skills. As the game is played, the SpeechViewer provides immediate feedback (visual, auditory, or both) and the child continues until the activity is complete. The hardware and software does all

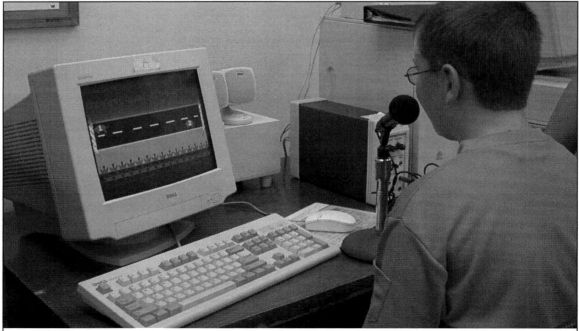

*Figure 10.1.* Student working on duration control using the IBM SpeechViewer III.

of this and generates a progress report while the child has fun playing a game. This system is available in Windows format only.

Several other companies have since ventured into the field of computer-assisted speech training. In 1978, Kay Elemetrics introduced a widely acclaimed system called Visi-Pitch. Like the SpeechViewer, the Visi-Pitch system operates off of a personal computer (PC). Both systems require additional hardware installation so that the software can be effective. The Visi-Pitch also helps a child develop the ability to articulate difficult sounds both phonetically and phonologically, modulate voice production, and produce vowels accurately. The software has components that allow the child to practice all of his suprasegmental speech skills as well as a component for dysarthria. Dysarthria is a speech production disability that involves a child's inability to produce sounds of speech voluntarily. The Visi-Pitch dysarthria component slowly and gradually encourages speech production through a series of physiological strategies that support articulatory production.

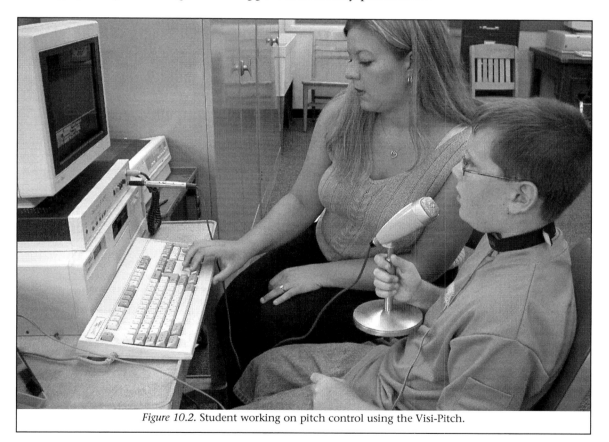

*Figure 10.2.* Student working on pitch control using the Visi-Pitch.

Two other recently introduced systems are The MicroVideo Corporation's VideoVoice Speech Training System and Communication Disorders Technology's (CDT) ISTRA (Indiana Speech Training Aid) system. Both of these systems operate on the same principle as the SpeechViewer and Visi-Pitch.

One of the drawbacks of many of these systems is the cost. Each system can potentially run into thousands of dollars, which is prohibitive for many school districts. Kay Elemetrics recently introduced a less expensive system, the Sona Speech Model 3600. This system can be used on a laptop computer with the standard sound card that is already present in most PCs today. It has all of the other instructional features of the higher cost instruments and it is portable as well.

## Computer-Generated Images

One of the most interesting, creative, and potentially groundbreaking items in the ever-changing field of technology is the use of **avatars.** An avatar is a three-dimensional, computer-generated figure that can be made to look like a person. Avatars are used for simulations and many other instructional applications. Signing avatars demonstrate American Sign Language (ASL) signs using all of the features of ASL: position, orientation, handshape, and direction. In addition, the avatars are able to use facial expression and body movement to accurately provide an almost real-life picture of ASL.

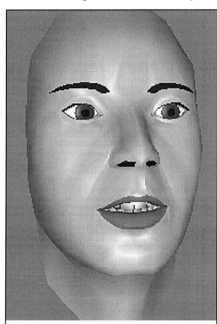

*Figure 10.3.* Baldi, a speech production avatar.

One of the most ingenious avatars is "Baldi." Baldi is to spoken language what signing avatars are to sign language. Baldi, a computer-generated "talking head," was developed by the University of California—Santa Cruz Perceptual Science Laboratory (http://mambo.ucsc.edu/) (Massaro, 1998). Baldi (Figure 10.3) is anatomically correct and produces speech that is nearly lifelike. As you watch Baldi talk, you can see accurate lip and tongue movements accompanying the speech production, which gives the impression that Baldi's speech sounds less synthetic. This is a significant improvement over other speech-synthesizing products. Baldi's face can be modified to show emotions or represent different ethnicities. The voice can emulate the pitch of a male, female, or child. Teachers can program Baldi to focus on targeted spoken language activities. Children have the opportunity to work individually or in teams interacting with Baldi to improve particular speech sounds or to enhance spoken linguistic abilities in general. Baldi can be used anywhere: in school, at home, or on a laptop.

Efficacy and usability research is being conducted with Baldi at the Tucker-Maxon Oral School in Oregon, and at a number of other schools. Preliminary reports indicate that Baldi has had a significant impact on the speech production of profoundly deaf children (Barker, 2001; Bosseler & Massaro, submitted; Stone, 1999). Other reports are available at the Tucker-Maxon School's website, www.tmos.org. The Baldi Toolkit is available for purchase from the Perceptual Science Laboratory.

# Speech Production Software

There are a vast number of speech production software programs available. The purpose of this section is not to endorse any particular software, but to enlighten the reader regarding the type of software available. In general, the speech production software available today attempts to develop both receptive and expressive spoken communication skills.

## Receptive Skills

The receptive tasks focus on each level of auditory skill development: awareness, discrimination, identification, and comprehension. In awareness tasks, a child must listen and indicate that a sound was heard. Discrimination tasks require that a child indicate a difference between the sounds that are heard. Identification tasks require that the child select a specific sound or statement, and comprehension tasks expect the child to respond to the software in a manner reflective of linguistic comprehension. Tasks are often focused on the principles of phonemic awareness. Many of these software products are found in both listening and literacy sections of product catalogues.

Some might question the purpose of using auditory-based software applications with children who have hearing loss. As we stated in earlier chapters, only the most profoundly deaf individual has no apparent residual hearing. The vast majority of children with hearing loss do have useable residual hearing. For most of those children, a major component of their Individual Education Plan is the development of those residual hearing abilities. Also, we cannot forget the severely profoundly deaf person who happens to be an auditory learner. Using this software enables the child to work on receptive communication skills in a relaxed and fun manner. There is nothing more boring to a child, teacher, or parent than labor-intensive drill-and-practice activities. The software activities are interesting, engaging, and reinforcing.

Earobics and Fast ForWord are two newer programs that show promise in the development of auditory perception skills. Both are computer-based software packages. Earobics focuses on increased phonological awareness, phonics training, and reading comprehension. The program was designed to assist students with disabilities who demonstrate difficulties with phonological awareness through practice and skills training. Fast ForWord is a program developed on the basis of recent findings in the field of neurolinguistics. Researchers believe that students with auditory processing difficulties require sound to be manipulated from a temporal or time framework in order to process the sound input accurately. This program changes the duration of the auditory input signal by lengthening certain attributes of the signal. The listener has a longer listening period of time and is then able to perceive differences in sounds that had been previously undetectable. Neither of these products was designed for students who are deaf or hard of hearing, but they have found their way into many programs for this population. Considerable research needs to be done with both Earobics and FastForWord in their application with students who have hearing loss. The potential for positive impact is possible for both of these programs.

## Expressive Skills

Expressive software focuses on the student's actual speech production and allows for guided modification and monitoring of both the segmental and suprasegmental components of speech. Expressive spoken communication skills software is the type discussed earlier in this chapter. The software that is used with SpeechViewer III, Visi-Pitch III, Sona Speech, and the other programs noted previously is representative of the activities found in most expressive communication software. Typically, a high quality microphone is used to record both the teacher and child's speech production. The student works at modifying his output to match the teacher's or the software parameters. All activities are completed in a gamelike format so that the child is provided constant feedback regarding his production. Feedback is both visual and auditory. As with the receptive software, students can work individually or in teams. The output targets are the same, regardless of the speaker.

Companies such as LinguiSystems and The Speech Bin have a large variety of computer-based products available for both receptive and expressive spoken communication development and enhancement. These companies, as well as others, are listed in Appendix C for your reference.

***Cued Speech.*** The National Cued Speech Association is the primary source for nearly all materials involving the development and use of Cued Speech. Several videotapes are available to learn and practice Cued Speech; these are appropriate for both adults and children. One of the most ingenious software items is *Cue That Word*, a Cued Speech program that enables a child to practice Cued Speech receptively and that ties the skill into a variety of phonemic awareness activities. Animations are used for each of the cuing activities. The child has control of the software. He can stop, review, respond, and review again. Each submitted response receives immediate feedback. The teacher can control the speed of the cue presentations. There is evidence that work with this particular software both enhances spoken communication skills and improves the phonemic abilities associated with reading and writing (Discovery, 2001–2002).

***Voice/Speech Recognition Software.*** Several speech recognition software companies produce software that can recognize an individual's speech pattern. One company, Sensory Incorporated, will customize avatars to meet the unique speech needs of any individual. This company allows the user to select or design a personal avatar, select the language (for non-English-speaking children, a very important modification), and provide a personal speech input model. The company then produces an avatar that is customized to the child and will recognize that child's speech input.

Another popular voice recognition product is *Dragon–Naturally Speaking 6*. This software, produced by Assistive Technologies, is designed to learn to recognize an individual's speech patterns. Once "trained," Dragon then transforms oral input to written output, allowing an individual a visual output mode of communicative efforts.

It would not be surprising if in the near future, speech recognition software becomes available for the deaf adult whose spoken communication skills are not clearly intelligible. This software might allow the deaf or hard of hearing individual to communicate orally and still be clearly understood by the hearing listener.

During a 1997 symposium on the applications of Automatic Speech Recognition with deaf and hard of hearing people, the participants both hailed the use of ASR (automatic speech recognition) applications and provided cautions as well. In addressing the ergonomic applications of ASR, Kathryn Woodcock (1997) warned, "We cannot just say we want an automatic speech recognition device to help with 'communication.' We want to target it to a particular category and we want to anticipate how smoothly a device would integrate into these different settings" (p. 48).

In the future, voice recognition software may indeed provide assistance to deaf or hard of hearing individuals who wish to use spoken communication in a variety of settings, but who may not have the intelligible speech skills to do so.

# Virtual Reality

Few students today have not had some exposure to the world of Virtual Reality (VR), or the sense of three-dimensional space in a two-dimensional activity. The advanced computer graphics engineering in the Nintendo Game Cube, Sony PlayStation, and Microsoft X-Box interactive game systems provide students with a sense of working the games in three dimensions. While entertaining, the opportunities for instructional applications are endless.

Pilots are trained using virtual reality simulators. Soldiers are trained in military science strategies using virtual reality simulations. In some medical schools, doctors are trained to perform some surgeries by first performing them in a virtual environment. There are even applications available that allow the dissection of a frog in a virtual biology lab. It is not unreasonable to expect that teachers will look toward virtual reality as an additional tool in their instructional tool bag. Currently, a virtual reality instructional system for D/HH students is being tested through the Florida School for the Deaf.

In this program, students are faced with a series of problems. Using the virtual reality headgear and joystick controller, the student navigates his way through the problems, making choices as he goes. The software provides feedback regarding the appropriateness of the strategies selected by the student to solve each problem.

**A VR problem-solving scenario:**

Student Problem: I have to get across a very busy intersection and there are no traffic signals. What strategies will I use to get across the street?

(The student puts on the VR headgear and holds onto the joystick. The student is now transported *into* a virtual three-dimensional scene where he has the choice to make certain decisions regarding the problem.)

VR actor: I can try to run across the street, beating the traffic that is coming. Let me try that.

(Result: The computer program will generate an automobile accident, a car swerving to avoid hitting the student, or perhaps a car hitting the student.)

VR actor: Yikes, wrong solution. Let me do that again and try another strategy.

Imagine the possibilities of using virtual reality in the development or enhancement of spoken communication skills!  From a phonetic to a pragmatic level of production, VR programs could be used to help students learn to monitor themselves more accurately and self-assess their abilities more clearly. Virtual reality is going to be a major force in instructional technology in the future.

# Speechreading

There is not much available in computer software applications for speechreading development and practice. The traditional form of practice material is written texts, and a few videotapes are available. The only computer-based source of material is *Speechreading Challenges on CD-ROM*. This CD-ROM program was created in 1998 as a joint project between the Education of the Deaf/Hard of Hearing Program and the Institute for Interactive Technology of Bloomsburg University. Dr. Samuel Slike, director of the Bloomsburg Education of the Deaf/Hard of Hearing Program, has noted:

. . . [T]his program was developed in response to requests from adults with hearing loss who could not find any technology-based materials available that gave them practice in their speech-reading skills. This instrument provides 11 chapters with different scenarios, 150 different faces, a variety of ages (from 4 years to 72 years), people from different ethnicities (Bangladesh, Brazil, Russia), and  provides a series of typical yet difficult speechreading contexts (stutterer, sucking a lollipop, cigarette, incomplete message models). Each chapter contains speechreading practice of 35–40 words, 20 sentences, and a short story related to the topics of the chapter.

*Speechreading Challenges on CD-ROM* is useful as a training tool for preservice teachers as well as a practice tool for deaf and hard of hearing individuals. As a training tool, it provides future teachers with an understanding of using speechreading as a communication tool and it sensitizes them to the challenges that D/HH individuals face when trying to speechread people from a variety of backgrounds. As a practice tool, currently used by children at or beyond the fourth or fifth grade level and adults, it provides an opportunity to practice speechreading before one of the scenarios is encountered. We can't always control who we are going to run into and what they are going to say. This was an attempt to give as much practice as possible to individuals who need to use speechreading as a receptive mode of communication. (Slike, 2002)

The *Speechreading Challenges on CD-ROM* program is good for current teachers as well. Pre- and posttest forms are available with the software, and each lesson can be monitored or facilitated by the teacher. The program has reportedly been successfully used with younger children who have cochlear implants (Slike, 2002).

When viewed within the context of our communication tool belt, speechreading abilities are an integral and important component of pragmatic-level spoken communication skills. *Speechreading Challenges on CD-ROM* is a groundbreaking endeavor toward meeting the needs of all individuals with hearing loss who would benefit from practice in speechreading skills. This unique software is currently available through Bloomsburg University and Harris Communications.

# Augmentative Communication Systems

A number of speech output devices are obtainable today to help a person use spoken communication if he is unable to produce speech. The way each of these systems works is similar. A core vocabulary is selected from software or is recorded using live voice. This vocabulary is saved as word, phrase, or sentence files. Buttons or a touch pad surface is used as a means of selecting linguistic output. Different statements are saved to each touch location. By simply touching that specific button or place on the touch pad, an individual is able to use the output device to speak for him.

Deaf and hard of hearing students rarely use this form of technology to communicate. However, it is important for teachers to be aware that such systems do exist, for those students who may have a severe motor disability and therefore, cannot use their speech, or communicate through sign language. Providers of augmentative communication systems are listed in Appendix C.

# Summary

Technology has the potential to significantly change the horizon for deaf and hard of hearing students. This chapter focused on the systems and software applications currently available that can assist in the development and enhancement of spoken communication for D/HH students. As members of a multidisciplinary team, it is important for us to recognize the types of activities that are available for our students. At the same time, we must be careful with those applications. Computer games are only as good as their developers make them. The successful use of technology in the development or enhancement of spoken communication skills is only as good as our applications of these systems and programs. It is important to remember that technology is only a means to an end, not the end in itself. We have repeatedly stated throughout this book that real human interactions and discussion are the keystones for any student developing the best possible spoken communication skills.

One of the greatest benefits to the use of computers is that the technology is available to the students throughout the school day and in many cases, also available at home. A word of caution, though: technology applications can easily become another form of the dreaded drill-and-practice routine. We must ensure that technology is truly used to enhance communications among our students rather than inhibit it. With the help of the latest technologies, spoken communication skills need not be relegated to a designated "speech period," but can be incorporated at any time throughout the day.

# Chapter 10 Topics for Discussion

1. Create a classroom lesson that incorporates at least two of the technology applications discussed in the chapter. Be sure to include your rationale for using your targeted technology, i.e., why is your idea better than doing the same thing without technology?

2. Predict the technology that might be available ten years from now and then twenty-five years from now. How will it change the face of spoken communication for deaf and hard of hearing students?

3. What other technologies have already changed spoken communication for D/HH students?

4. You have just been hired to open a new resource classroom for the deaf and hard of hearing children in a tri-county area. Your supervisor wants a list of the technology tools you want for your classroom. Create that list and state the reasons for your selections.

5. Your students are in the middle of an exciting game using the Visi-Pitch when the computer crashes. What low-end technology might you use to complete the activity?

*Appendix A*

# Anatomical Drawings of the Hearing and Speech Mechanisms

## Anatomy of the Hearing Mechanism

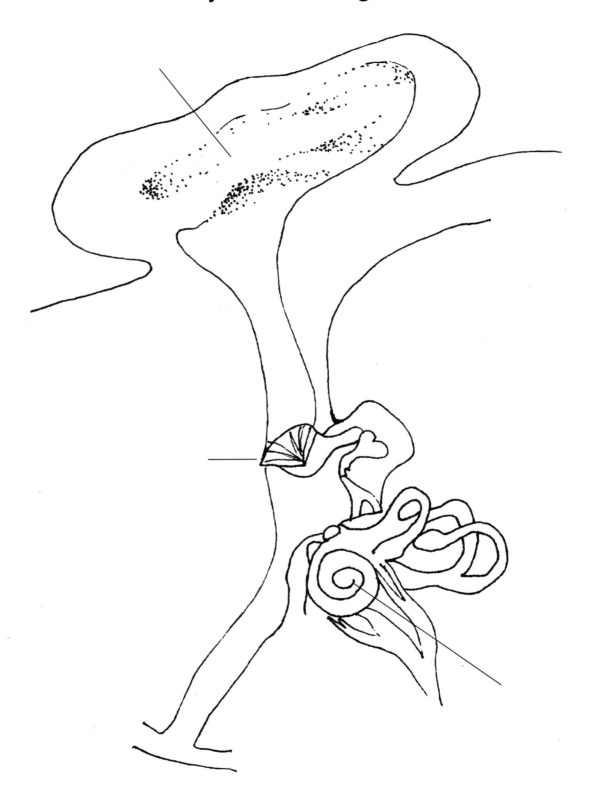

# The Outer Ear

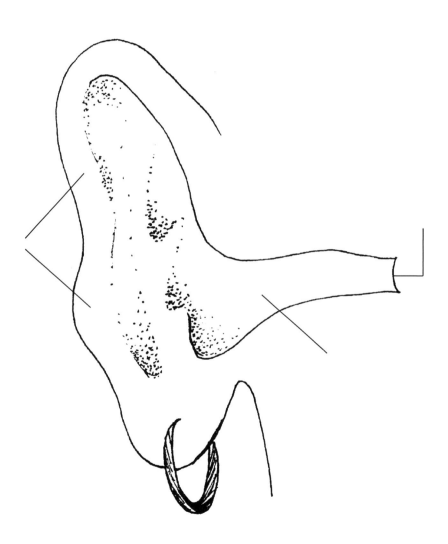

# The Middle Ear

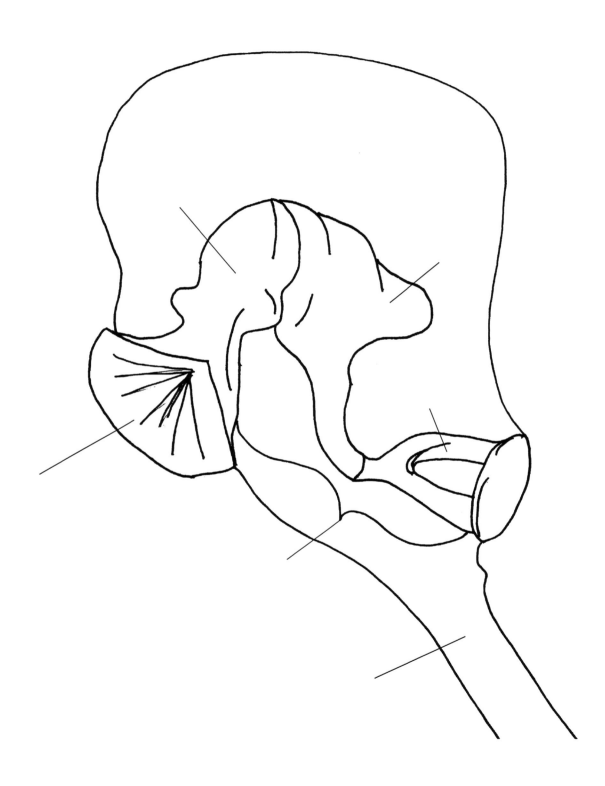

# The Inner Ear

# The Neural Pathway

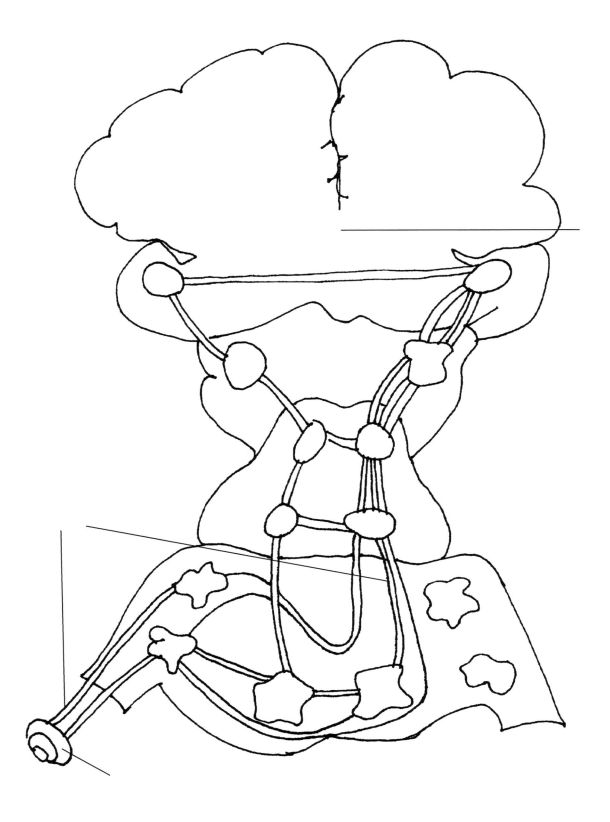

# Lateral View of the Speech Mechanism

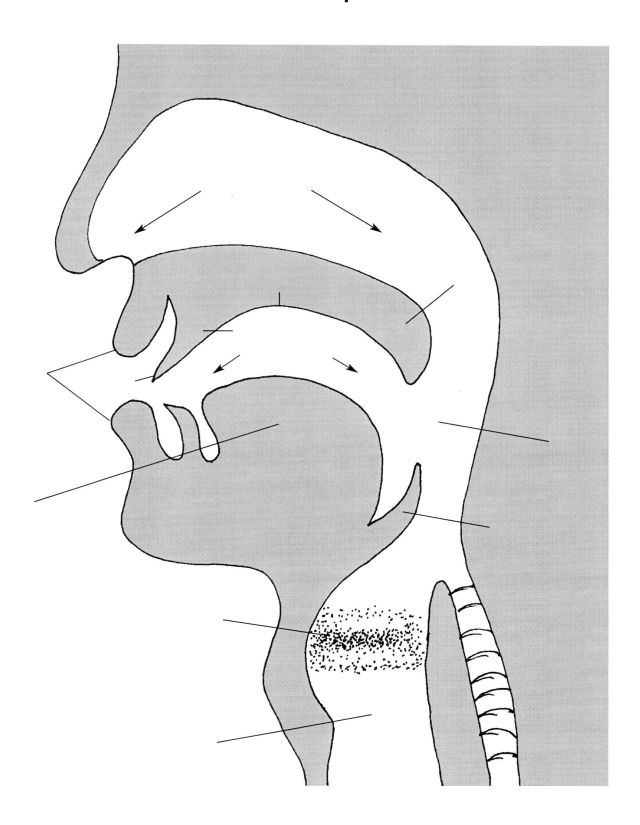

*Appendix B*

# Informational Websites Related to Hearing Loss

A.G. Bell Association for the Deaf and Hard of Hearing
http://www.agbell.org/

Amarillo Independent School District Support Services
Regional Day School Program for the Deaf
www.amarillo.isd.tenet.edu/deafed/default.html

American Annals of the Deaf
http://gspp.gallaudet.edu/annals/

American Society for Deaf Children
http://www.deafchildren.org/

American Speech-Language-Hearing Association
http://www.asha.org/

The ASHA Leader
http://professional.asha.org/publications/leader.htm

Audiologist Online
http://www.audiologistonline.com/

Auditory-Verbal International, Inc.
http://www.auditory-verbal.org

Better Hearing Institute
http://www.betterhearing.org/

Classroom Acoustics Resource Guide
http://www.classroomacoustics.com/

Clarion Corporation
http://www.cochlearimplant.com/

Cochlear, Ltd.
http://www.cochlear.com/

Cochlear Implant Association, Inc.
http://www.cici.org/

Convention of American Instructors of the Deaf
http://www.caid.org

The Council for Exceptional Children
http://www.cec.sped.org/

Deaf Education Website
http://www.deafed.net

Deafology 101
http://deafology.com/

Directory of National Organizations of and for Deaf and Hard of Hearing People
http://clerccenter.gallaudet.edu/InfoToGo/184.html

Earinfo
http://www.earinfo.com/howread.html

Hearing Health Magazine
http://www.hearinghealthmag.com/

Infant Hearing References for Auditory Screening
http://www.colorado.edu/slhs/mdnc/ref_screening.html

Information and Advocacy for People Interested in Hard of Hearing Children
http://www.hardofhearingchildren.com

The Journal of Deaf Studies and Deaf Education
http://deafed.oupjournals.org/

National Association of the Deaf
http://www.nad.org/

National Cued Speech Association
http://www.cuedspeech.org

National Information Center on Deafness
http://clerccenter.gallaudet.edu/InfoToGo/index.html

Noise Pollution Clearinghouse
http://www.nonoise.org/quietnet.htm

Perspectives in Education and Deafness
http://clerccenter.gallaudet.edu/products/Perspectives/index.html

Public Broadcasting System
www.pbs.org/wnet/soundandfury/cochlear/cochlear_flash.html

Self Help for Hard of Hearing People
http://www.shhh.org/

SKI-HI Institute
http://www.skihi.org

System of Universal Verbotonal Audition Guberina
http://www.suvag.hr

*Appendix C*

# Vendors of Instructional Materials and Assistive Devices

ADCO Hearing Products
5661 South Curtice Street
Littleton, CO 80120
(800) 726-0851 V/TTY; (303) 794-3928 V/TTY
http://www.adcohearing.com/

American Sign Language Videos
Gene Grossman's MAGIC LAMP PRODUCTIONS
1838 Washington Way
Venice, CA 90291-4704
(310) 822-2985; (800) 367-9661
http://www.aslvideos.com/

Animated ASL Dictionary
http://www.bconnex.net/~randys/index1.html

ASL Access
http://www.aslaccess.org

Auditech – TTY and Assistive Devices for the Deaf and Hearing Impaired
P.O. Box 821105
Vicksburg, MS 39182-1105
Voice/TDD: (800) 229-8293
http://www.auditechusa.com/

Butte Publications
P.O. Box 1328
Hillsboro, OR 97123-1328
Phone/TTY: Toll Free: (866) 312-8883; Direct: (503) 648-9791
http://www.buttepublications.com/

> **Note:** The Oral Peripheral Examination Form and the Student Speech Record
> are available separately from Butte Publications.

Communications Unlimited
9618 Oregano Circle
Houston, TX 77036
Relay: (800) 735-2988
TTY: (713) 271-7818
http://www.communltd.net/

DawnSign Press
6130 Nancy Ridge Drive
San Diego, CA 92121-3223
TTY/Voice: (858) 625-0600
http://www.dawnsign.com/

Deaf Resources
http://deafresources.com/

DEAFWORKS
http://www.deafworks.com/

Dragon-Naturally Speaking
http://shop.voicerecognition.com

Edmark
Riverdeep Inc.
125 Cambridge Park Drive
Cambridge, MA 02140
(617) 995-1000
http://www.riverdeep.net/edmark/

Gallaudet University Press
800 Florida Ave. NE
Washington, DC 20002
TTY/Voice: (202) 651-5488
http://gupress.gallaudet.edu/

Harris Communications, Inc.
http://harriscomm.com/

HearMore
42 Executive Boulevard
Farmingdale, NY 11735
Voice: (800) 881-4327
TTY: (800) 281-3555
http://www.hearmore.com/

IBM SpeechViewer III
http://www-3.ibm.com/able/snsspv3.html

John Tracy Clinic
806 West Adams Boulevard
Los Angeles, CA 90007
(213) 748-5481
http://www.jtc.org

Kay Elemetrics
http://www.keyelemetrics.com

LightSPEED Technologies
15812 SW Upper Boones Ferry Road
Lake Oswego, OR 97035
Pro Audio and Sound Field: (800) 732-8999
http://www.lightspeed-tek.com/

LinguaSystems
http://www.linguisys.com/

Discovery
National Cued Speech Association
23970 Hermitage Road
Cleveland, OH  44122
(800) 459-3529
http://www.cuedspeech.org/

Mayer-Johnson, Inc.
P.O. Box 1579
Solana Beach, CA 92075
(800) 588-4548; (858) 550-0084
http://www.mayer-johnson.com/

Pro-Ed
8700 Shoal Creek Boulevard
Austin, TX 78757
(800) 897-3202
http://www.pro-ed.com/

Scientific Learning Corporation
300 Frank H. Ogawa Plaza
Suite 500
Oakland, CA 94612-2040
(888) 665-9707
http://www.fastforword.com/

SIGNhear Communication Center
http://library.thinkquest.org/10202/

Slosson Educational Publications, Inc.
P.O. Box 280
East Aurora, NY 14053
(800) 828-4800
http://www.slosson.com/

Speech Bin
1965 Twenty-Fifth Avenue
Vero Beach, FL 32960
(800) 4-SPEECH (800-477-3324)
http://www.speechbin.com/

SRA/McGrawHill
http://www.sra4kids.com/

Super Duper Publications
(800) 277-8737
www.superduperinc.com

Ultratec
450 Science Drive
Madison, WI 53711
(608) 238-5400
http://www.ultratec.com/default.html

Video Voice
Micro Video Corporation
P.O. Box 7357
Ann Arbor, MI 48107
(800) 537-2182
http://www.videovoice.com

ZYGO Industries, Inc.
P.O. Box 1008
Portland, OR 97207-1008
(800) 234-6006
http://www.zygo-usa.com/

*Appendix D*

# Communication Book Inserts

Dear Parents,

I'm so glad that you've agreed to enhance your child's opportunities for spoken communication by doing the activities in this book! I hope that it will be a fun and rewarding experience for both of you.

You will find that I have included five sections of different activities for you and your child to look at for ten or fifteen minutes each night. You may choose any one activity to practice speech and other English language skills. Please contact me right away if you have questions or concerns about these activities.

## Directions

1. Find a comfortable place to work.

2. Start by reviewing an activity that your child really enjoys.

3. Introduce the new activity and follow the directions on the page.

4. Give lots of praise and support for your child's efforts.

5. Complete the activity with your child, remembering to give him as many opportunities as possible for success.

6. Close the book after fifteen minutes unless he begs you for more! Give him a hug a and a big pat on the back! ☺

# Make a circle around all of the words that **begin**

# with the letter *b.*

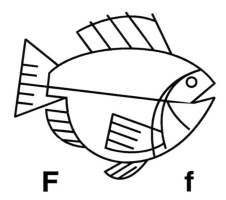

**F          f**

1. Say the sound five times.

2. Say the sound in a word.

3. Write three more words with this sound:

_____

_____

_____

4. Find or draw pictures for each word.

5. Practice writing the letter:

_____

- - - - - - - - - - - - - - - - - - - - - - - - - - - - - - - - - - - - - - - - -

_____

# Polly the Pig

I have a pink pig,
a pretty, pink pig,
a pretty pink pig, you see.
When I pet my pig,
my pretty pink pig,
some pennies come out for me!

1. Underline the words that begin with *p.*
2. Make a purple circle around Polly the Pig.
3. Draw a penny next to Polly.
4. Read the poem about Polly out loud to your parent.

**Name**_____

**This week's spelling words are:**

1. _____

    Sentence _____

2. _____

    Sentence _____

3. _____

    Sentence _____

4. _____

    Sentence _____

5. _____

    Sentence _____

6. _____

    Sentence _____

7. _____

    Sentence _____

8. _____

    Sentence _____

9. _____

    Sentence _____

10. _____

    Sentence _____

**How many syllables are in each word?**

**Underline the words that have the /s/ sound.**

**Circle the words that end in *-ing*.**

Read this short story and complete the activities at the end.

**Molly loved to read, so she went to the library to borrow a new book. Molly's teacher wanted the kids to get a "mystery" for their next book report. Molly asked the librarian where she could find the best mystery books. She decided to get the book with the scary-looking cover, because she loved to get scared! Molly couldn't wait to get home to read the new mystery.**

1.    Who was the girl in the story?

      _____

2.    Where did she go to find a book?

      _____

3.    What kind of book did she need to borrow?

      _____

4.    Why did she choose the book that she did?

      _____

5.    Underline all of the words that begin with *m.*

      _____

6.    Say all of the *m* words aloud.

      _____

7.    (Trick) Find the word where the /m/ sound comes at the end.

      _____

# Write your own story using the following words:

mom    milk    money    my

me    matter    mine

more    mine

magic    middle    monkey

_____
(title)

# Some Ground Rules (for the older student)

So, you want to get the most out of your communication efforts?  In order to do that, there need to be some basic ground rules before we begin.

**1. Choose a "monitor."**

A monitor can be anyone you can work with productively.  Examples of a monitor are mother, father, uncle, aunt, brothers, sisters, or responsible friends.  The monitor does not have to be the same person each time.

**2. Choose a quiet place to work.**

A desk or table will be helpful.  Turn off the TV or radio, unless your assignment requires it.

**3. Agree on the amount of time you will work.**

This amount can change from time to time based on homework or other neces- sary events that come up.  When you have agreed on the amount of time, that entire time must be devoted to communication.  Do not accept interruptions of any kind.

WHO is your monitor?  _____

WHERE will you work?  _____

HOW MUCH TIME?  _____

Now that you've set your ground rules, *enjoy* the many communication opportunities open to you!

# A Message to the Student

This book is intended to help you practice your spoken communication skills. You made a good choice by wanting to improve this aspect of your communication abilities.

Everyone sets goals for himself or herself. Your teachers, friends, and parents have certain goals that they want for themselves. A goal is something you want to achieve. A goal in sports would be to improve your batting average, or to take off seconds in a race. A goal in school might be to maintain a "B" average on a report card, or to stay up-to-date on homework.

By agreeing to work in this Communication Book, you made a goal for yourself: to improve your spoken communication skills. You have made an excellent choice! When you have more tools available, you will find it easier to make new friends, get a job, succeed in college or in a job, and better understand the world around you. Congratulations on a great decision.

When you set a goal for yourself, you must be committed to achieving it. It will take hard work and practice, just like the sports and schoolwork goals. Don't get discouraged, and have fun!

# Favorite TV Show

A. With your monitor, watch one of your favorite TV shows together. One half-hour sitcom is best.

B. When the show is over, turn off the TV and discuss the show together.

C. Using your speech and speechreading only, have your monitor ask you some questions about the show.

       Examples:

          1. Who is the main character?

          2. What was the main idea of the story?

          3. Where does the show take place?

          4. What was your favorite part of the show?

D. After answering these questions, ask your monitor some questions of your own.

Name of the show? _____

In the space below or on a separate piece of paper, write a short summary about what you discussed and bring it to school.

# Making Introductions

A.  You know the steps in making a good introduction.   Let's review them here:

    1.  Make eye contact.

    2.  Be polite.

    3.  Repeat the person's name after you're introduced.

B.  Write down what you'll need to say to make a good introduction.  Some statements are included here, and you may add more if you like:

    1.  _____, I want you to meet _____.

    2.  _____, this is _____.

    3. Hi, _____.

    4. It's nice to meet you.

    5.

    6.

    7.

C.  By yourself, practice saying each of the phrases above.

D.  With your monitor, practice saying each of these phrases.

E.  Perform a "mock" introduction.  (Pretend you are meeting someone for the first time.  Also, pretend to introduce people who don't know each other.)

F.  Sometime this week, make an actual introduction.

G.  Write one paragraph describing how your introduction went.

# Interviewing

## Purposes:

1. To learn how to ask questions

2. To listen to answers

3. To learn more about others

## Directions:

1. Conduct an interview once each week.

2. Begin with various monitors.

3. As you feel more comfortable with interviewing, try it with new people.  For example, you could interview a friend of your parents', a neighbor, or a person whom you met at a party.

4. How many questions can you think of to ask the person?  On a separate piece of paper, write as many questions as you and your monitor can think of together.  When you're all done, each of you thinks of two more questions.  Then when you're really all done, circle the eight best questions.

5. Do you think you'll get better answers by asking "yes/no" questions, or other questions?

6. Write down the "question words" you can use.  (There should be at least five).

7. Practice.  Before you do an interview, practice these two things:

    a. Have your monitor cover up your page of questions.  How many can you remember?

    b. Role-play the interview with your monitor.  Pretend he or she is someone else, and practice the interview.

*Appendix E*

# Sheet Music: *When I Sing La La La*

# When I Sing La La La

When I sing la, la, la, then you sing *(children)* (la, la, la). If I

change la, la, la, then you change (la, la, la). If it's

high la, la, la, you sing high (la, la, la). When it's

low la, la, la, then you go (la, la, la). Hear a

scale la, la, la, la, la; sing a scale (la, la, la, la, la). Com-ing

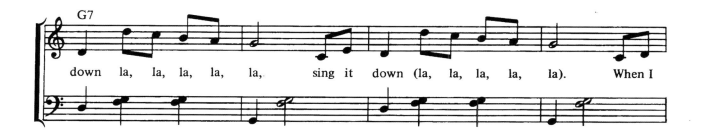

down la, la, la, la, la, sing it down (la, la, la, la, la). When I

skip la, la, la, then you skip (la, la, la). Add a

*Appendix F*

# Handouts Facilitating Parent Involvement

## Multidisciplinary Team Survey

As a valued team member, please fill out this survey.  I would like to know how you rate the importance of each member of the team.  I want _____ (student's name) to have the best year possible and I feel confident we can achieve this, if we all work together.

In what ways can the following team members contribute?  Specifically, what can each person do?  How do you see the strengths of these team members?

Classroom teacher:

Teacher of deaf and hard of hearing children:

Parent:

Student:

Speech Specialist:

Dear Parents,

I am so glad that you have agreed to be a partner in your child's education this year. There are many ways you can help.  Please read the opportunities listed below and rank them in the order that you feel you can help.

If you can commit to this on a regular basis, give it a **1**.

If you can commit partially, give it a **2**.

If you cannot commit to this, give it a **3**.

_____     Help my child with homework

_____     Work with my child four nights each week for ten minutes on the
             Communication  Book

_____     Come to the class to work in centers once a week for one hour

_____     Come to the class to work in centers once a month for one hour

_____     Participate in phone calling (as needed)

_____     Volunteer on field trips

_____     Help with bulletin boards

_____     Help with special projects

_____     Other ideas?  Please explain. _____
             _____

Do you have any special talents that you could share (art, music, storytelling, crafts, other?)

_____

_____

Thank you for being a team member!

Classroom Teacher_____

Parent name, phone number, e-mail _____

_____

# Teacher Checklist for Parent Volunteers

When a parent agrees to become an active team member, be sure to ask yourself the following questions:

1. _____    Did you give the parent every opportunity to volunteer?

2. _____    Did you make the parent feel like a valued team member?

3. _____    Have you given the parent responsibilities with which he or she feels comfortable?

4. _____    When the parent comes to the classroom, will you introduce him or her as a team member?

5. _____    Do you have detailed plans for the parent volunteer to follow?

# *References*

Association Method. (2002). [On-line]. Available: http://www.awcoslo.org/Sections/AboutUs/gift_of_speech.htm

Auditory Verbal International, Inc. (2000-2001). [On-line]. Who...what...when...where...why? Retrieved March 23, 2002, from http://www.auditory-verbal.org

Barker, L. J. (2001). Computer-assisted vocabulary acquisition: The CSLU vocabulary tutor in oral-deaf education. Journal of Deaf Studies and Deaf Education, in press.

Beiter, A., & Brimacombe, J. (2000). Cochlear implants. In J. Alpiner and P. McCarthy, Rehabilitative audiology: Children and adults (3rd ed.). (pp. 473–496). Baltimore: Lippincott Williams & Wilkins.

Bosseler, A., & Massaro, D. W. (submitted). Development and evaluation of a computer- animated tutor for vocabulary and language learning in children with autism. Journal of Autism and Developmental Disorders.

Brady, J. (1977). When I sing la la la. In Watch Me Sing. Salt Lake City, UT: Brite Music Enterprises, Inc.

Bunch, G. O. (1987). The curriculum and the hearing-impaired student: Theoretical and practical considerations. Austin,TX: Pro-Ed, Inc.

Calvert, D. R., & Silverman, S. R. (1983). Speech and Deafness (Rev. ed.).Washington, DC: A. G. Bell Association for the Deaf.

Candlish, P. A. (2000). [On-line]. Ling 5 or 6 Sound Test. Available: http://hardofhearingchildren.com/Great%20Information/ling_sound_test.htm

Dillon, H. (2001). Hearing aids. Turramurra, Australia: Boomerang Press.

Discovery. (2001–2002). The Bookstore of the National Cued Speech Association. Cleveland, OH: NCSA.

Easterbrooks, S. R., & Baker, S. (2002). Language learning in children who are deaf and hard of hearing: Multiple pathways. Needham Heights, MA: Allyn & Bacon.

French, M. M. (1999). Starting with assessment: A developmental approach to deaf children's literacy. Washington, DC: Pre College National Mission Programs.

Gelfand, S. (2001). Essentials of audiology (2nd ed.). New York: Thieme Medical Publishers, Inc.

Graney, S. (n.d.). Where does speech fit in? Spoken English in a bilingual context. Sharing Ideas Series. (Available from Laurent Clerc National Deaf Education Center, Product Inquiries, National Deaf Education Network, KDES PAS 6, 800 Florida Avenue, N.E., Washington, DC 20002).

Interactive Learning Styles Test. (2002). [On-line]. Available: http://www.ldpride.net.

International Communication Learning Institute. (1988). <u>Visual phonics.</u> Edina, MN: ICLI.

Johnson, H. (2002). <u>U. S. deaf education teacher preparation programs: A look at the present and a vision for the future.</u> Manuscript submitted for publication.

Klein, D. H., & Glor-Scheib, S. (2001). <u>Delivering special education support services: Voices from the field.</u> Unpublished manuscript, Indiana University of Pennsylvania.

Kroth, Roger L. (1975). <u>Communicating with parents of exceptional children: Improving parent-teacher relationships.</u> Denver, CO: Love Publishing Company.

Levine, M. (2002). <u>A mind at a time.</u> New York: Simon & Schuster.

Ling, D. (1976). <u>Speech and the hearing-impaired child: Theory and practice.</u> Washington, DC: A. G. Bell Association for the Deaf.

Ling, D. (1989). <u>Foundations of spoken language for hearing-impaired children.</u> Washington, DC: A. G. Bell Association for the Deaf.

Lowell, E. L., & Stoner, M. (1960). <u>Play it by ear! Auditory training games.</u> (Available from John Tracy Clinic, 806 West Adams Blvd., Los Angeles, CA, 90007).

Marshall, S., Nussbaum, D., & Waddy-Smith, B. (1999). Kendall School integrates literacy skill development with auditory and speech services [Electronic version]. <u>Perspectives in education and deafness, 17,</u> Retrieved March 17, 2002, from http://clerccenter.gallaudet.edu/Products/Perspectives/may-un99/marshall.html

Marschark, M. (1997). <u>Raising and educating a deaf child</u>. New York: Oxford University Press.

Massaro, D. W. (1998). <u>Perceiving talking faces: From speech perception to a behavioral principle.</u> Cambridge, MA: MIT Press.

McGinnis, M. A. (1963). <u>Aphasic children: Identification and education by the association method.</u> Washington, DC: A. G. Bell Association for the Deaf.

Moores, D. F. (2001). <u>Educating the deaf: Psychology, principles, and practices</u> (5th ed.). Boston: Houghton Mifflin Company.

Nicolosi, L., Harryman, E., & Kresheck, J. (1996). <u>Terminology of communication disorders: Speech-language-hearing</u> (4th ed.). Baltimore: Williams & Wilkins.

Northern, J., & Downs, M. (2001). <u>Hearing in children</u> (5th ed.). Baltimore: Lippincott Williams & Wilkins.

Nover, S. M., & Andrews, J. F. (1998). <u>Critical pedagogy in deaf education: Bilingual methodology and staff development.</u> Santa Fe, NM: New Mexico School for the Deaf.

Ordway & Janke. (1992). <u>The adventures of Superman.</u> New York: DC Comics.

Otis-Wilborn, A. (1992). Developing oral communication in students with hearing impairments: Whose responsibility? Language, Speech, and Hearing Services in Schools, 23, 71–77.

Palmer, J. M. (1993). Anatomy for speech and hearing (4th ed.). Baltimore: Williams & Wilkins.

Parker, E. W., & Koike, K. J. M. (1984, June). Musical stimulation in speech training for hearing-impaired children as utilized at the Utah School for the Deaf. Paper presented at the meeting of the Japanese Verbotonal Society Conference, Tokyo, Japan, and The Alexander Graham Bell Association for the Deaf Convention, Chicago, IL.

Schimmel, C. S., Edwards, S. G., & Prickett, H. T. (1999). Reading? Pah! (I got it!) Innovative reading techniques for successful deaf readers. American Annals of the Deaf, 144, 298–308.

Schirmer, B. R. (1994). Language and literacy development in children who are deaf. New York: Macmillan Publishing Company.

Schirmer, B. (2001). Psychological, social, and educational dimensions of deafness. Needham Heights, MA: Allyn & Bacon.

Slike, S. (February 23, 2002). Personal communication.

Stewart, D. D., & Kluwin, T. N. (2001). Teaching deaf and hard of hearing students: Content, strategies and curriculum. Needham Heights, MA: Allyn & Bacon.

Stone, P. (1999). Revolutionizing language instruction in oral deaf education. In Proceedings of the International Conference of Phonetic Sciences, San Francisco, CA. Retrieved March 30, 2002, from http://cslu.cse.ogi.edu/toolkit/pubs/index.html

University of California—Santa Cruz Perceptual Science Lab. (1998). Baldi/Toolkit. Retrieved June 5, 2001, from http://mambo.ucsc.edu/

van Uden, A. (1970). A world of language for deaf children: Part 1. Basic principles (2nd ed.). Rotterdam, Netherlands: Rotterdam University Press.

Verbotonal Method. (Retrieved 2002). [On-line]. Available: http://www.suvag.hr

Vestibulocochclear Nerve. (Retrieved 2002). [On-line]. Available: http://www.faculty.washington.edu/chudler.neurok.html and http://www.faculty.washington.edu/chudler.cranial.html

Wilson-Favors, V. (n.d.) Using the visual phonics systems to improve speech skills: A preliminary study. Retrieved February 19, 2000, from http://www.casagrande.com/~icli/usingvp.html

Woodcock, K. (1997). Ergonomics of applications of automatic speech recognition for deaf and hard of hearing people. In R. Stuckless (Ed.), Frank W. Lovejoy Symposium on Applications of Automatic Speech Recognition with Deaf and Hard of Hearing People (pp. 41–54). Rochester, NY: Rochester Institute of Technology.

# *Index*